OVERCOME

How I Miraculously Healed from a Fractured Neck

DOMINICK GIACOBBE

Copyright © 2024 Dominick Giacobbe
All rights reserved
First Edition

PAGE PUBLISHING
Conneaut Lake, PA

First originally published by Page Publishing 2024

ISBN 979-8-89315-495-5 (pbk)
ISBN 979-8-89315-504-4 (digital)

Printed in the United States of America

The Eagle symbolizes bravery courage and immortality, able to face challenges, and overcome obstacles. The Eagles keen eyes keeps him safe and protected.

Contents

Preface vii
Introduction ix
To Overcome xv

Chapter 1
    How I Fractured My Neck 1
    Mental Toughness 8
    The Impossible 14
    A Miracle 18
    Mind Power 20
    Developing Mind Power 25

Chapter 2
    Never Accepting Defeat 28

Chapter 3
    My Doctor 35

Chapter 4
    Making the Plan 39

Chapter 5
    The Road to Recovery 45

Chapter 6
   Treatment for Success..55
   The Study 60

Chapter 7
   Life after a Near-Death Experience....................................68

Chapter 8
   Conclusion..72
   My Seven Miracles or Near-Death Experiences in My Life ...77

Preface

I wrote this book to be an inspirational tool for anyone facing odds that are unbelievable. I hope that after reading this book, you will look at life differently. I hope that on the journey of your life, if you are ever faced with a major challenge or an impossible situation, the knowledge you gained from this book will help you approach it with a positive, determined mind. You will learn how to face your challenges and conquer them. I hope that through my journey, you can learn how to use the power of believing to reach your dreams and goals.

In this book, I will explain how I went from everything to nothing and back to everything. How I went from being one of the most respected Korean martial artists in the world to being in the hospital bed with a fractured neck, unable to move. This book is my journey back from a broken neck to becoming a full-time martial artist again. I am a very determined and disciplined person. I have always faced my challenges in life with the strength to overcome and conquer them. Each challenge prepared me for the next one. I learned that, in a lifetime, you will be faced with many challenges, and the most successful people overcome most of their challenges. At a young age, when I played sports, I learned how to be strong and how to overcome my injuries, pains, and weaknesses. I developed a never-quit attitude, and I learned how to overcome my fears. We all have these amazing powers, but most of us never learn how to develop or use them.

Introduction

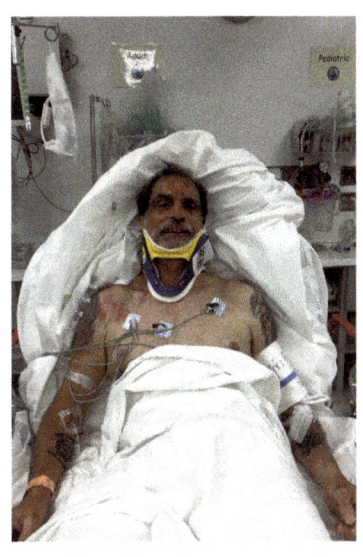

This was me the next day after the motorcycle accident. My neck was fractured in three places, and my body was severely bruised.

    Growing up in New York City prepared me for life and many of its challenges. It was a tough environment, which taught me how to take care of myself and how to be strong. When I was sixteen years old and in my junior year of high school, my family moved from New York City to southern New Jersey, about fifteen miles from Philadelphia. This was a tough move, changing all my friends and acquaintances. It was like I had to start over again in life. I was challenged by some of the tough kids in the new school, and I had to protect myself in the conflicts. I was not accepted by any of the athletic coaches because I was from New York, and I was also not liked because I had long hair. I had played sports in school since I was a young boy, and now I was not even getting a chance to show my talents. I was always the kid who worked the hardest and played with the most enthusiasm. I did all the sports and was always loved by my coaches. However, I was now faced with a totally different situation. In my senior year of high school, I played no sports. However, I still did my running because I had a love for running since I ran on the track team from the seventh grade to the eleventh grade.

After I graduated from high school, my brother was killed in action in the Vietnam War. I was very troubled by this and was very confused. I did not know if I should enlist, go to Vietnam, and get revenge for his death, or if I should take my brother's advice to stay away from the service. In my brother's last letter to me, he told me, "No matter what, do not join the service. This is a horrible place to be. Nobody wants us here. We are fighting a war with no purpose." He stressed how there were so many deaths for nothing. He wanted me to take his advice and do whatever I could to never come to Vietnam. His advice was very convincing because I looked up to him. He was my hero. He was two years older than me, so we were together my whole life. When the news came from the army that he was killed in action, I first went into denial and would not believe it. I just thought it was all a big mistake and he would come home, but that never happened. Now I had to face it and say to myself, *This is life, and in life, there is death.* I was very angry at the world and the government for sending my brother there. I had so much on my mind. I do not know how I got through this troubled time. Soon after his death, I decided to join a karate school—Shin Karate Institute. This changed my life. It put me back into a physical training routine that I was used to from all the sports training I did for so many years. It also created new positive challenges, and it took away my anger and hurt feelings. Karate taught me how to face my weaknesses and how to stay focused on reaching my goals. After each class, I felt great. I was very inspired to become great at martial arts. I worked very hard, training five to six classes per week. In my mind, I said that I was doing this for my brother, Angelo Giacobbe. Karate was very motivating and challenging.

OVERCOME

I went on to obtain my black belt, and I began competing in tournaments and national martial arts events. I developed a very successful reputation. I opened a karate school in 1974 and continued growing in my abilities. I would dedicate four to five hours a day to intense physical fitness. I went on to become a nationally recognized martial artist. I appeared in national magazine articles and on the covers of five international martial arts magazines. I appeared on over a hundred TV shows and news programs, developing a strong reputation by demonstrating the amazing powers of the mind. In the year 2000, I was inducted into the Black Belt Magazine Hall of Fame. This is the highest honor a martial artist can achieve.

After forty-eight years of training and teaching the Korean martial art of *Tang Soo Do*, I had a severe motorcycle accident that fractured my neck. I went from being one of the most talented martial artists in the world to not being able to do anything. It was quite frustrating to go from everything to nothing. However, when the doctor told me that I would never do martial arts again, I was very determined to prove him wrong. I never had a negative thought. In my heart, I knew that I would conquer this. In this book, I will explain how I went from nothing to everything. I will explain all my ups and downs and how I used my mind to overcome the impossible.

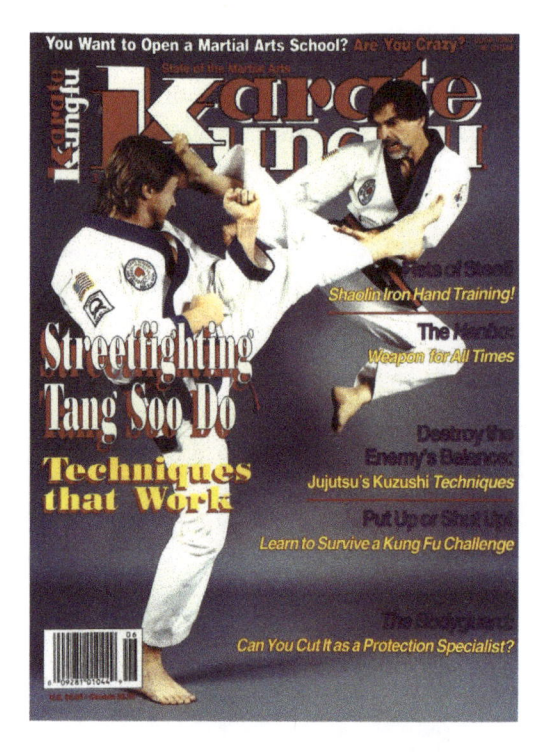

OVERCOME

Be a person who has the will to conquer and overcome. The inner will is the strongest weapon in the world. (D. A. Giacobbe)

To Overcome

To overcome is the power that is developed within you to conquer and be victorious in whatever battle confronts you. To overcome is to be able to face your challenges with strength and determination. You must maintain a powerful mind with no negativity. Focus on how you will be victorious and work hard to reach your goals. Develop a never-give-up attitude and believe in yourself. To begin, you must plant the thought, "I can get through this." Yes, you must keep thinking, *I can get through this.* When I was first diagnosed with a fractured neck, I was devastated. I refused to believe that I was in jeopardy of having a stroke and being paralyzed from the neck down. It was horrifying and quite scary. It was nothing like I was ever faced with, but I just kept saying, "I will get through this." I said this many times a day, never ever giving up on myself. To overcome this, it requires true focus and hard work.

I will get through this.

We can overcome this by using the power of positive thoughts, which will develop mind power. You must learn how to direct your thoughts and how to keep all thoughts strong, powerful, and positive. It's like climbing a mountain. To climb a mountain, you begin by planting the thought that you will get to the top of the mountain. If you think that you will climb halfway and see if you can reach the top, you will never make it to the top of the mountain. You must have only one thought: *I will reach the top of the mountain.* Next, you start your journey. Just keep focused on getting to the top. Never look down. Just stay strong and keep climbing. These are the kinds of thoughts that you must develop to have the power to overcome them. Overcome is a powerful word. It challenges you; it pushes and scares you, but it gives you strength. To overcome is to be strong, powerful, and victorious.

To develop the power to overcome, you must flood your mind with positive thoughts and your final goal. You must make a plan and stick to it. Keep telling yourself, *I can get through this.* Stay strong by not allowing negative thoughts to change your mind. Face small roadblocks on your journey with powerful thoughts and be focused on your final goal. In martial arts, we say, "Never retreat in battle well. In developing the power to overcome, you must have the attitude that you will fight to the end and never give up, no matter how hard it gets." So begin your journey to overcome by saying, "I can get through this."

Chapter 1

How I Fractured My Neck

Dominick Giacobbe and wife Angela with the Harley-Davidson

My 2008 Harley-Davidson Fat Boy

It was the hottest day of the summer—Sunday, August 13, 2016. On this hot, sun-filled day, we decided to take a ride on my motorcycle. My motorcycle was a Harley-Davidson Fat Boy. I had been riding motorcycles since 1968. I was considered a very experienced rider. I asked my girlfriend, Angela, if she wanted to take an afternoon ride in the countryside of New Jersey. It was such a beautiful, hot day. We decided to go for a ride. We both had our helmets on and left for our ride. In New Jersey, there is an area called the Pine Barrens, which is a one-hundred-square-mile area of preserved pinelands in which there are no houses or buildings. The Pine Barrens is a very beautiful part of New Jersey, with little traffic and nice country roads. Riding a motorcycle in beautiful, glowing areas is a form of meditation. You feel nature, air, and wind. It is a feeling of freedom.

As we were riding along the country road, traveling about fifty miles per hour, in a split second, a car pulled out of a stop sign, blocking my lane. As he pulled out, there was a car coming in the opposite direction, causing both cars to stop and present a roadblock in front of me. Apparently, he never saw me on the road. In a split second, I hit my breaks, and the bike started sliding sideways. As the bike was skidding, I thought of my cousin Emil Donofrio, who was a motorcycle police officer in Hoboken, New Jersey. I remembered him telling me about his training for riding motorcycles and how he stressed what you should do if you were confronted with a crash. I remembered how he said that it is much safer to lay your bike down than to hit an object head-on. I remembered how, in his training, he had to ride the motorcycle thirty miles per hour, then lay it down. It was funny that, although all of this was happening in a split second, it was going in slow motion for me. I was not sure if everyone had these feelings of everything slowing down in an instant before a tragedy or whether it was from all my many years of martial arts training.

In that split second, I realized that there was no way that I could stop and no way that I could get around the car, so I laid the bike down. I remember throwing the bike down and raising my arms to protect me from the crash that was about to happen. In an instant, I hit the car on the driver's door. I turned my head to the left, hitting my face on the door. My girlfriend, Angela, was saved by my actions. By laying the bike down, we stayed together, and she did not fly off the bike. My body protected her from hitting the car directly and allowed her to escape the accident with very minor injuries. At the point of contact, I remember the crunching sound of hitting the car with my face and head. We were both thrown to the ground and lay in the center of the road.

At first, I felt like an elephant was lying on my body. I could not move anything. It was a weird experience. I was totally aware of the situation, but it was like I was spiritually separated from my body. Although I remembered my complete conversation with Angela and the other people around me as I lay on the pavement, I could never remember being on the ground. In an instant, I could not move any part of my body. I do not know if I was temporarily paralyzed or if I was unconscious. I remember analyzing my injuries. I knew I had hurt the right side of my neck. I could feel it was injured because I had a piercing pain from the neck to the head. I also felt bad pain in my left shoulder and my right ribs. As I lay there, I first began moving my toes, then my fingers. I was beginning to get the feelings back from my mind into my body. I knew I did not want to move anything, so I stayed in that position very still and just concentrated on my breathing. The most apparent thing to me were my teeth. I knew a few of my teeth were knocked out. I had blood in my mouth and nose, making it hard to breathe.

However, as I lay there, I felt that feeling of safety come over me. I knew I was going to be okay. I had that feeling of safety during other times in my life when I had other near-death experiences. It's a feeling of being protected from being seriously injured or dying. Soon after the crash, the police arrived, and within five minutes, the ambulance was there to assist me. The paramedic asked me where I felt the pain, and it was funny because I quickly responded, saying that it was at my right neck, my right ribs, my left shoulder, and my mouth. They then put a plastic brace around my neck, put me on a stretcher, and carried me to the ambulance. As I was getting into the ambulance, the medic asked me what year it was. Wow! I was so dizzy that I really couldn't remember. I was thinking, *Is it 2015?* But at that minute, I just couldn't put it together. Then he asked who the president was. I quickly responded, "Oh, it's Obama." Then my mind became clear, and I then began to feel all the bruises over my entire body. At this point, I had good movement of my limbs and no restrictions on movement, just a lot of pain.

The ambulance arrived at the hospital, and I was quickly brought into the emergency room. The nurses and doctors began to analyze my injuries and said that before they did anything, I would need a CAT scan. They brought me to the X-ray room and did the CAT scan. I was then taken back to the emergency room. Soon after, my daughter Kimberly and her husband, Christian, arrived. I was happy to see them. I told them that I was okay and that there was no need to worry. Then my sister Barbara arrived, and she was so worried about me. I started thinking that I was worse than I thought. It was because of their reaction to my condition. Angela, my girlfriend, was by my side, and I thought she should have the doctors check her out because we were both thrown on the ground going fifty miles per hour. She was very scared for me, but she had an injury to her elbow.

As I lay there for an hour, the doctor came to my room, and I asked, "What is the result of the CAT scan?" He advised me that the hospital had nobody to read the scan and that it was on the internet, waiting for a doctor to analyze it. I was shocked that it took over an hour to have it analyzed. After an hour and a half, the doctor came to me and said that it was read by a doctor in India. My neck was seriously fractured in three places, and they could not treat me there. They said I had to be transported to a trauma hospital. They asked me if the pain was too bad for me to be taken by an ambulance. If so, they would transport me via helicopter. I told them that I was okay to go in the ambulance.

The ambulance arrived, and the two most amazing ladies attended to me. I was in the hospital for over two hours, and nobody did anything. I had blood all over my face and in my nose. It was difficult to breathe. The two ladies cleaned my face and nose, so I was able to breathe again. They got me ready for the trip. It was about fifty miles to Cooper Trauma Hospital, so they gave me a shot of a powerful painkiller. As a student of martial arts for so many years, I had never taken any pain medication my entire life, nor did I drink any liquor, so I was totally numb from the morphine pain medication I was already on, and then they gave me a shot of fentanyl for the dangerous drive. They put me in the ambulance, and we went on an hour-long drive to Cooper Hospital in Camden, New Jersey.

We arrived at Cooper, and it was so different from the first hospital. They had seven people working on me, checking every part of my body. They did an ultrasound, checking my organs and doing a very intense inspection of every part of my body. They said I needed another CAT scan because the one from the previous hospital was not clear. The second CAT scan revealed that my neck was broken in three places. C1 was fractured, and the bone was separated. C4 and C5 were also fractured, and a piece of the bone was also separated. They said C1 was very dangerous, and I had to be very careful not to move at all because it could slip, and I could have a stroke and either die or be paralyzed.

They decided to do another CAT scan of my entire body to see if I had any other injuries. Good news: no other broken bones, organs were all intact, and everything else was working fine. After the second CAT scan and several evaluations of my condition, the doctors decided to do a third CAT scan of my face to see if I had any other broken bones. The examining doctor said that I was very lucky to be alive with the fracture I had in my neck. I was thinking that it wasn't luck. I knew that I survived the crash because I was a trained martial artist and that, in a time of emergency, my mind and body adapted to the situation, and I survived.

I believe that there is a spiritual or internal power within all of us that protects us. However, most people are not in tune with their spiritual selves, and they do know how to tap into this special power. I believe my spirit took over and saved my life. This spiritual power is developed through meditation and disciplined physical training. As my occupation was as an instructor of the martial arts, I spent years studying meditation and mind development. Disciplined physical training (DPT) is physical training that requires your full mental concentration and focus for at least one hour continuously. This type of training will enhance your spiritual powers. When a student of martial arts is training in class, they are challenged mentally and physically, forcing the student to have full focus and concentration. If you think about it, martial arts classes were developed by the monks thousands of years ago. It is believed that the monks designed the martial arts not only for self-defense and protection but also as a means of spiritual development. The monks encircled their activities with the development of the spiritual self and internal energy. They practiced meditation for hours each day. They spent time in nature, relaxing, and practicing martial arts. All these activities led to a person with amazing spiritual abilities. I remember one of my instructors telling me that I should sense danger before I see it. He said that it is being in tune with your spiritual self. So I am positive that I was not as lucky as the doctors and nurses said I was. However, I was sure that there was some luck involved. Who knew? It might have been a miracle.

OVERCOME

I remained in the trauma area for several hours. I was constantly analyzed by the nurses. I had all kinds of things hooked on me. I was under intense surveillance. I was then transferred to the intensive care unit for the next twenty-four hours. I had a personal nurse with me, constantly making sure that I had no complications.

The first night was very hard to get through. I was uncomfortable and in extreme pain. I had body aches, injured bones, and an injured nose, causing limited breathing, aching teeth, and severe rib and shoulder pains. The mental pain was also troubling, as was the fear of not being able to do my regular martial arts routines ever again. Every hour, the nurse came in to check my vital signs and temperature. I was only drinking liquids, and I had to lie perfectly still, flat on my back, on an inclined bed with this very uncomfortable plastic neck brace. I could not sleep at all. I was so tired and hurting all over. I began thinking that I would get through this. That night, I focused my mind on healing from the accident.

The next day, they moved me to a regular room. They said I could eat a regular meal; I was so hungry. I felt like I had not eaten for a week. I ordered all kinds of foods, like chicken and potatoes. Well, to my surprise, I was unable to eat any of the solid foods because all my teeth were knocked loose. I lost two teeth; two teeth were broken in half; and the rest were all loose. I was able to eat soft foods like oatmeal and liquid drinks. This was horrible. I never experienced having a problem like this. All my front teeth felt like they could just fall out. I had ice packs on my shoulder and my ribs, and I also kept icing my gums, trying to help strengthen my teeth. I was upset about my teeth, and I was more upset because I could not eat solid foods. The next day was even worse. My body was so sore that I could not touch any part of it without it hurting. I was totally bruised from head to toe.

Besides my hurt neck, the very uncomfortable neck brace, and my loose teeth, I had extreme pain in my left shoulder. I must have torn the shoulder muscle on contact with the car. I could not lift my left arm at all. When I wanted to move my left arm, I had to use my right hand to lift my left arm. Whenever I had to move my left arm,

I had serious pain. My right ribs were also bruised very badly, causing pain when I took deep breaths.

My deepest concern was not the pain. It was whether the fractured neck would end my martial arts future and change my life. I had a strong inner feeling that I was going to heal from this. I knew that if I survived the accident, then I could overcome whatever I may be faced with. I just put the positive thought in my mind that I would overcome this obstacle. Even though my mind was very positive, I had that huge fear of being paralyzed or being unable to function as a normal person.

A Sunday motorcycle ride to New Hope, Pennsylvania

Every day is a challenge. Prepare for it, face it, and overcome it. Challenges are there to be conquered. Strong people find a way to overcome their challenges. What challenges us makes us stronger. (D. A. Giacobbe)

Mental Toughness

Mental toughness is the most important tool to motivate your spirit and inner strength. In *Tang Soo Do* Korean karate, learning techniques, training, and obtaining belts are mental and physical challenges that present goals that you must conquer. Developing a powerful inner self is important to accomplish these tests, as each higher test gets more difficult and more challenging. There is no room for error. If you do not perform correctly, you will have to retest. Developing mental strength is at the core of all martial arts training. Karate develops mental toughness and physical strength, which give the student focus and determination to conquer whatever he or she may be faced with. To overcome the impossible, you will need mental toughness.

In my experience, I have great respect for martial artists and boxers. They have amazing mental strength, and they train hard to develop it to its fullest potential. Back in 1985, I had a karate school in Hollywood, California. While teaching there, I met Sugar Ray Leonard. We became friends, and he asked me to attend a fight in Las Vegas between Roberto Duran and Marvin Hagler. At that time, I was teaching his personal bodyguard, James Anderson. I was an assistant bodyguard for the weekend with Sugar Ray Leonard and James Anderson. We were at the ringside for the fight because Ray Leonard was the HBO commentator. As the fight progressed, Ray was excited. After the fight, Ray said, "I can beat Hagler." He saw something and had an intuition that he could beat him. However, Hagler was a middleweight, and Ray was a welterweight. Hagler was much bigger and stronger. Ray said to me, "If I get a fight with Hagler, I want you to come to the camp and teach me some of the mind stuff. He said he always had an interest in karate.

Sure enough, about eight months later, I got a call that he had secured the fight. Ray Leonard was a huge underdog since he did not have a fight for a long time due to a detached retina in his eye, but the doctor gave him the "okay" to fight again. This was a display of physical strength versus mental strength. Ray worked hard at getting under Hagler's skin. We set up camp near Boston, which was Hagler's hometown. That bothered Hagler. Ray kept doing things to make Hagler mad. We trained vigorously. It was a great experience. We got up each day at about 5:00 a.m. We ran four or five miles, then I put him through a tough physical workout, working on speed and developing punching power from the hips. He was very eager to do anything to give him an edge in the fight. Each afternoon, he spent about two hours in the boxing gym, doing rounds on the bags and doing rounds with sparring partners. This was a great experience for me. I got to be with the famous boxing trainer, Angelo Dundee, each day. I learned so much about boxing and the strategies of fighting. Our goal was to have Ray Leonard know all Hagler's weaknesses and have him mentally prepared to conquer him. Each night, we watched films by Hagler. We watched his weaknesses and developed a plan of attack. Ray was extremely confident, although everyone thought he was going to get knocked out in the first round. After eight weeks of training, we went to Las Vegas for the fight. It was a great fight. Hagler was very frustrated and wanted to kill Leonard. This worked against him. Ray was methodical and just stuck to the plan and kept scoring points. As the fight went on, Hagler got madder and madder, and this allowed Ray to beat him. After the fight, I thought of how mental strength conquered physical strength. We were all overwhelmed with the success of the fight. Sugar Ray Leonard was a true example of a person with extreme mental strength.

OVERCOME

Another fight that displayed the power of the mind was the Ali Forman fight. Forman was a huge man, a true powerhouse. He was knocking each of his opponents out. Forman was also a huge favorite in the fight. However, Ali did the rope a dope, took a pounding for seven rounds, and when he sensed Forman getting weaker, Ali turned it on. Ali had nothing left. He was hurting all over. He reached into his mental strength and somehow got enough energy to reverse the odds and knock Forman out. Ali was an amazingly strong person. I knew him from many years before, when he first won the boxing title. We were friends, and he was an amazing athlete. I always enjoyed being around him. He displayed a strong, positive mind and lots of confidence. These boxers have the power of the mind instilled into their way of life.

After the Ray Leonard Hagler fight, I was asked to train many other boxers. What I learned from working with Ray Leonard was very valuable for working with other boxers. I was hired by world-famous boxing trainer Lou Duva to help train the five Olympic champions. They were Evander Holyfield, Mark Breland, Meldrick Taylor, Pernell Whitaker, and Tyril Biggs.

Four of the five became world champions. I enjoyed working with Holyfield. He was a great person, very dedicated, and a very hard worker. My job was to get these five guys into top physical and mental shape to help develop them into world champions. I worked with each of them for their first five fights, and I was brought back when they all had a championship fight. I worked hard on developing their mental strength. I often refer to the Hagler-Leonard fight and how Ray beat Hagler mentally.

As a teacher and a person who works with the mind, I have great respect for people with mental toughness. I understood that without mental toughness, you can never conquer your challenges. Many of the boxers I worked with used the power of their minds to overcome the impossible. Since my life was all about the mind and developing it to its highest potential, when I was personally confronted with being mentally tough to conquer my fractured neck, I thought, *I have talked the talk for many years, and now I will walk the walk.* I thought, *I will overcome the impossible.*

Through the years of training karate, I began practicing meditation. I was taught by my teachers that mental strength is developed through meditation and through hard physical training. As I developed in the martial arts, I also gained strength of mind and mental toughness. Many experiences in life will either make you mentally stronger or discourage you and weaken you. A strong positive attitude will help convert your experience from negative to positive. I remember my dad saying that whatever you may be faced with can be a lot worse, so don't be negative. Face your challenges, be strong, and conquer them. Learning about the mind and its powers was my goal as an instructor of *Tang Soo Do*. I wanted a strong mind and worked very hard to obtain it. I began performing feats of the mind and soon became known as the mind master. I walked on broken glass and pulled a truck with my teeth. I pierced my arms with motorcycle spokes, hung buckets of water from the spokes, and controlled my bleeding. I was in total control of my mind, and I was accomplishing feats that were unbelievable. I performed all around the world, showing the people that we all have this amazing power. It's called the mind. Now I would be determined to use all that I learned to conquer my fractured neck. I was on a mission.

In my life, I have always surrounded myself with strong-minded people. My karate masters had powerful minds and strong discipline. They were great examples for me to follow. When I worked with the Philadelphia Eagles football team, I had the great opportunity of working with defensive end Reggie White. He was amazing—the best NFL defensive end in the history of the league. His amazing abilities were derived from the amazing power of his mind, which gave him enormous strength and discipline. While Buddy Ryan was the coach of the Eagles, he had the defense train karate with me for three months each offseason. I taught the players moves with their hands and many techniques of leverage. Reggie worked hard and had the power to believe. Reggie was making moves against opposing teams and adding his mental toughness. He was unstoppable at times. In an NFL football game, it was like being in a battle; you fight with the player across from you. So when I was teaching the Eagle players karate, I was also teaching them about mind power and how to develop it. We did karate training and ended each class with meditation. I loved working athletes of this caliber. They all had strong, powerful minds to get to where they were. I worked with the Philadelphia Football Team players for twelve years.

Grand Master D. A. Giacobbe was pictured here with NFL defensive end Reggie White, one of Master Giacobbe's karate students.

The Impossible

Impossible, not able to occur, no chance to accomplish, nonexistent, cannot be done, an undoable task, or just physically impossible—these are the meanings of impossible. I'm sure that in all our lives, we have faced impossible situations. However, with the right tools and philosophy, the impossible can be overcome. Overcoming the impossible begins with the mind. It begins with one single thought—a seed. Once the seed is planted, you must make it grow. The power of believing will give you a special power to accomplish your feat. Discipline and determination will be the other tools that will be needed to make the impossible possible.

In the martial arts, the power of believing is one of the most important factors in being successful. We learn techniques, practice them, and believe that they will work. The power of believing makes martial arts possible. For example, in breaking boards or cement blocks, the first and most important thing is that you must believe that you have the strength and power to break the object. We say it means seeing through the object. We break the boards or blocks first with our mind, then we can break them with our body.

I remember an old story about the power of believing. It is an old martial arts story. It is about becoming a master archer. The story is about a young man who dedicated his life to becoming a master archer. He had a great master who was his teacher. He did vigorous exercises daily and practiced with the bow for hours. He would practice on the run, on a horse, and in many different positions. He became an expert after many years of dedicated hard work. The teacher then told the young archer that if he wanted to be a master archer, he would have to go to the jungle and face a tiger. He would have to kill the tiger with his arrow. This feat would show his abilities as a master and overcome his fears and emotions. The teacher told him that he must believe in his powers and abilities to be victorious. So one night, the young man sharpened his arrows, checked his bow, and set out to accomplish this amazing feat. He had fears, knowing some old stories of other warriors finding the tiger and being killed by the tiger. But his determination to become a master gave him special power and confidence.

It was a cold, lonely, and fearful feeling, but he washed it away with the powerful thought of believing. He worked his way to the area where the tiger was likely to be. He picked a spot in front of the clearing. Behind the clearing was a small mountain of rocks. So the young archer waited for the moment to face the tiger. He heard a noise. He focused his mind on the area in front of the mountain wall and saw an image. He began to see the outline of the great tiger. He picked up his bow and aimed his arrow. Knowing the strength of the tiger, he pulled the arrow back farther than ever before. He focused his eyes on the spot and let it go. He heard the arrow hit, and then it was completely quiet. He sat there for several minutes and decided to go back to the camp and return in the morning to see the dead tiger. He did not tell his master because he wanted to be sure that he killed the tiger.

The next morning, he went back to the spot, and to his surprise, there was no tiger. Instead, his arrow was stuck firmly into the rock. He sat down and put his head down in shame and sorrow. Then his master suddenly arrived and told the young man to stand up. He told him to pull the arrow out of the rock. He grabbed the arrow but could not pull it out. The master said, "Show me the spot where you shot the arrow from." The young man went to the spot. The master handed him the bow and an arrow. The master told him to shoot the arrow into the rock. He shot one arrow, and it flew off. He then shot several arrows, but they all flew off. The master said, "It's the power of believing. Last night, when you truly believed that the image was a real tiger, you focused your mind, your body, and your spirit, and at that point, you had enormous power to believe. Today, you cannot make the arrow penetrate the rock because you do not believe that there is a tiger there." The master then told the young man to follow him. They went to another spot on the mountain, and there was another arrow in the rock. The master said, "That is my arrow, and it is my tiger. I congratulate you on becoming a master archer. You demonstrated true strength, focus, and belief. You now understand the power of believing."

In this old story, we truly understand the power of believing. So to overcome the impossible, you must truly believe and use the power of believing. To conquer the impossible, you must plant the seed of belief and keep believing.

OVERCOME

The power of believing makes the impossible possible. (D. A. Giacobbe)

    Discipline is also very important because, to overcome the impossible, you need discipline. Overcoming the impossible is usually a difficult feat to accomplish. As you can understand, true discipline is strongly required. There are two types of discipline. One is physical, and the other is mental. Mental discipline means not allowing your mind to create any negative thoughts. Whatever you are faced with, you must have discipline to keep yourself positive and strong. You need your mind to be 100 percent. You need to be mentally positive. Physical discipline is when you overcome something physically, and you do not allow your body to overcome your mind. Physical discipline is fighting pain and overcoming it. Pain is a single or subtle physical notice to notify the mind that there is a problem. However, through meditation, breathing, and mental training exercises, you can turn the pain off. In my experience, when I was dealing with my fractured neck and neck brace, many days I would wake up with strong pain and stiffness. I would just go about my daily actions and fight it off, and sooner or later, I would overcome it and feel no pain. Through my whole recovery, I never took any pain medicine or any opioid medicine. The discipline I learned in martial arts classes was guiding the way for me.

Determination is the ability to continue to pursue something with strong emotional motivation. We say that determination is the fire in our eternal spirit. It is the energy, or chi or ki, that motivates our spiritual selves to pursue our dreams and never give up. In *Tang Soo Do* karate, we develop strong determination, working hard to achieve our belts and degrees. Determination is what connects the mind, body, and spirit. With the right determination, you can accomplish anything. Determination is what drives you to find success and gives you the inner power and positive energy needed to conquer the odds. Being determined means being strong, positive, and focused. Determination is the discipline that leads you to where you are going and knows how you are getting there. To overcome the impossible, you will need very strong determination and the will to pursue your goals.

Work hard. Stay dedicated, and success will follow. Be determined to reach your goals, and do not let anything distract you. Goals are obtained through positive thinking, discipline, and determination. (D. A. Giacobbe)

A Miracle

A miracle is the effect of an extraordinary or amazing event in the physical world that surpasses all known human or natural powers and is described as a supernatural cause. It is also such an amazing event that it is manifested or considered a work of God. A miracle is a wonder or a marvel of life. It is overcoming the unbelievable. It is also the surpassing of an ordinary event that is beyond belief. It is an event that cannot be explained.

Miracle is the word often used to characterize any beneficial event that is statistically unlikely but not contrary to the laws of nature. It is surviving a natural disaster or simply a wonderful or amazing occurrence bringing results of the extraordinary. It is beating the odds or overcoming the unbelievable. Other miracles may be the survival of an illness diagnosed as terminal, escaping a life-threatening situation, or "overcoming the odds."

A true miracle is a nonnatural phenomenon, leading many rational and scientific thinkers to dismiss them as physically impossible. A miracle is the breakdown of established laws of physics within their domain of validity. It is impossible to confirm its nature because all possible physical mechanisms can never be ruled out.

A miracle is also viewed as a divine act of God. A miracle is an unusual or mysterious event that is thought to have been caused by God because it does not follow the usual laws of nature. When you read the Bible, it speaks of all the amazing miracles that Jesus performed. Many people cannot believe the miracles that he performed. Miracles are a part of life. How they happen and why they happen, I guess we will never know.

However, I ask, "Is a miracle a miracle, or is it just luck?" Although luck plays a strong role in miracles, I am sure it is not luck alone that develops miracles. Do miracles just happen, or can we make miracles happen through the will to survive, hard work, determination, or our inner strength? Every day, we hear of miracles, and we always question if it was a miracle or not. Since I experienced my own personal miracle, I am a believer. I personally believe that miracles are a divine act of God. It is God's way of letting all humans know that there is a God, and he is looking over all of us. You may or may not believe in God, but these miracles that happened to me are unexplainable. When science cannot explain a miracle, it must be a divine act. After you experience a true miracle, you become a believer in miracles.

This book is not about God. It is about my personal experiences that, in most people's eyes, are true miracles. It is about how I have experienced several miracles in my life and how they have changed me in many ways. This book will explain how I survived a serious fractured neck, how I was able to overcome the odds, and how I was healed from the injury. I am sure that each one of us has experienced some sort of miracle in one way or another for ourselves or for someone we know. However, when the miracle is a life-deciding miracle, then it is a true miracle.

Here, Master Giacobbe is demonstrating mind power in Italy.

Every miracle began as a problem. (D. A. Giacobbe)

Mind Power

You will need the power of your mind to be able to overcome your challenges, especially the impossible. Mind power is the tool that will give you the opportunity to find success in your battle against the impossible. Mind power is learning how to direct the mind in a positive way.

What is mind power? Mind power is the mind working to its highest potential. It is going beyond its normal capabilities. It has the power to overcome human restrictions. It is the power of intense concentration. It is to overcome bodily pain, the ability to stay focused without distraction, and the power of extreme discipline. It is the ability to have a sixth sense that enhances the ability to know things before they happen, and it is the ability to feel without seeing. Mind power is the key ingredient in overcoming the impossible.

It is known that humans do not use the full potential of their minds. Through the development of mind power, you will learn to use more of the mind and enjoy the many benefits of this power. Through the development of mind power, we will develop the use of more of the mind and, in turn, use more of its healing powers. Mental exercise is what helps us develop the mind to its fullest potential. If we think of a human as a train, we can say that the human body is the train, while the engine and driver are the mind. A train can be in great condition with a powerful engine and beautiful looks, but without a driver, it will not move. The mind is what makes us work. It controls our every action and makes us who we are. When we go through life, we will learn many things and have many experiences. However, developing the mind to its fullest potential will enable us to overcome the impossible.

Grand Master Dominick Giacobbe was pulling a van
with his teeth, demonstrating true mind power.

Mind power was understood centuries ago when monks and warriors searched for methods of developing a higher degree of concentration and awareness. A monk wanted mind power to reach the enlightenment of the spirit. The warrior wants mind power to give him an edge in combat. When life was simple, people looked within for power, not to computers or easy methods of advancement. Mind power is something that takes years to develop. It is developed through meditation, relaxation, breathing exercises, physical fitness, concentration techniques, maintaining a healthy diet, and a healthy lifestyle that is free of stress and anxiety. Mind power is a gift resulting from hard, disciplined work. It is the ability to overcome pain and depression. It is being positive and having positive thoughts. It is the power of believing in your thoughts and trusting your mind in a positive direction. It is your mind having complete control over your emotions.

Mind power is the ability to separate your emotions from your actions. It is making good choices that will lead to good results. It is having a strong and positive personality and a mind that will never be conquered. The mind is controlled by you and by your thoughts. When you are strong and confident in your thoughts, you will be strong and confident in your actions. The mind is the strongest tool in the universe. Learn to use it, and you will enjoy the many benefits. Mind power is the ability to sense things before they happen. It is having a sixth sense in life. It is the ability to communicate on a different level in life. It is the ability to trust your feelings and know when danger is present. It is the ability to feel when you are in a positive environment. Mind power develops the ability to be well-balanced, calm, peaceful, safe, confident, and comfortable. In *Tang Soo Do*, we call this *Pyung Ahn*.

Every human will enjoy these benefits, but how many will dedicate themselves to developing them? It takes years to develop mind power, but the benefit of experiencing life to a higher degree is the reward. This leads to happiness from within through your feelings of confidence and awareness. You will not be burdened by pain and weaknesses. You will have strength and comfort. The mind is the road to health and happiness. If you do not use it, you will lose it. The mind will grow weak and unproductive if it is not challenged and developed. All humans have this power. However, it is like a diamond; a diamond must be polished to shine. Developing mind power requires hard, dedicated work.

The first step to developing mind power is education. It is learning all about the mind and how it functions. You must first have a complete understanding of the mind and how it works. You must understand the different parts of the mind and their functions. You must believe in yourself and believe that you have the strength to develop this unique power. Once you fully understand the brain, you can begin to do the different exercises for mind power. In this book, I will lead you through my experiences of how I used mind power to overcome the impossible and how I cured myself of a very serious injury. You have the ability to use your mind to overcome the impossible. Just follow me on the journey into the development of the mind.

When a person develops mind power, they also develop a sixth sense. As you may already know, we have five senses: seeing, smelling, tasting, feeling, and hearing. Through mind power, you will be able to develop your sixth sense. You will have the ability to feel the spirit. Many monks call this developing the third eye. It is the ability to feel without touching. It is the ability to feel danger or distress before it happens. You will be able to tell when a certain place is good for your spirit or bad. Warriors need to feel danger before it happens, so they are not surprised when confronted by the enemy.

My sixth sense saved my life in the motorcycle accident, adjusting my body to absorb the impact of the accident and preventing me from dying. I knew I was injured, but I also knew that I was going to survive and that, in time, I would be back to normal. I had this feeling from the very beginning, and it never left me. I believe it was my inner spirit, giving me the momentum and mind power to heal and overcome.

To develop this power, you must begin by paying attention to your feelings. The first thing you must learn is to develop the feeling of being in a positive and healthy environment. When you feel your environment is comfortable, it is usually a good place for you and a good place for your mind. If you feel your environment is uncomfortable, then it is not good for you to be there. Our outer environment is like the water in a fish tank. If the water in the fish tank is clean and pure, the fish will live a healthy, long life. However, if the water is dirty and unhealthy, the fish will grow ill and die. Our environment is our water, so we must remain in a good environment to be healthy. When we have a healthy environment, our mind will function at its fullest potential. By learning to trust your feelings and spending as much of your life in a healthy, positive environment, this will aid in developing the sixth sense, which is very important in the development of mind power.

Monks and students of meditation find a special place to meditate. Some monks have searched for years to find a special place for meditation. It is a custom to always meditate in the same place. This is because when you meditate in the same place over a long period of time, you will develop a positive energy field in that room, which will be a healthy environment for your mind. If you spend many hours in this energy, you will feel strong positive energy. When you are confronted with negative energy, your mind will send signals to your body of discomfort. This is how the sixth sense is developed.

Meditation is an exercise for the mind. It is like the push-ups of the mind. To develop the power of your mind, you will have to learn how to meditate and develop this special power. Meditation is done by sitting in a quiet and comfortable place. Close your eyes and relax. Try to create a calm and peaceful scene in your mind, like a calm lake of water. Allow your mind to free itself from all your worldly thoughts. Breathe softly and feel the calmness that develops from quietness. At first, it may be hard to clear your mind, but with discipline and continued work, soon you will feel the energy through your body and a calming of your mind.

To develop mind power, you will have to change your way of thinking. Using your mind and all its powers will change your thoughts and actions. This change will lead to new experiences that will lead you to a better and stronger life. Our thoughts are controlled by our mind, so make strong, positive thoughts and trust your mind. Mind power will be one of the most important tools to overcome the impossible.

Developing Mind Power

Many people ask me how I developed mind power. It all began when I was sixteen or seventeen. I heard about meditation in stories about India and the Middle East. I was interested in learning but had no path to it. When I was eighteen, I joined *Tang Soo Do* Korean karate training. As a student, I began seeing the high-ranking masters perform amazing feats that could only be performed with mind power. This excited me. I wanted to learn all about mind power. I often asked my teacher how I could learn this. He told me to sit in a quiet place, close my eyes, relax, and reflect on my daily experiences, discarding all negative thoughts and accepting all the positive feelings, and then I would feel my spiritual self.

The next step would be to try this meditation and see if I could find this magic power. Each day, I sat in a quiet place, learning how to relax and how to adjust my thoughts for a clear mind. The meditation used in karate is like a Zen meditation. It is clearing the mind of all thoughts and allowing the body to relax, giving a feeling of floating. In karate, we say that this develops the spirit. Karate is the development of the mind, body, and spirit. You must learn how to combine these different powers into one balanced line of communication. For example, you must use your mind to develop your body. You must relax your body to develop your spirit. When your body becomes exhausted, your spirit will take over. By the time I was a green belt, I was working on meditation.

My first task with my mind was to break a board with my bare hand. I was instructed to relax and take a breath to calm my inner self. Focus on the center of the board. Imagine going through the board, then yelling, uniting the mind, body, and spirit, and hitting the board. When everything is right, your physical technique, mental focus, and spiritual power from within will lead you to success. My first task was a success. I broke the board. Soon after, I tried two boards and continued till I broke five boards. As I entered the red belt, I began breaking cement blocks. With each harder material I used, my mind and focus had to get stronger.

When I was a senior red belt, I set a goal to break a red brick with a chop. Well, red bricks are extremely hard, and because the size is so small, it is a very difficult break. However, I was very determined to break the brick. I began using my mind to imagine hitting the brick and seeing it break. Finally, I decided to give it a try. I set up a station with two cement blocks used as a stand to support the red brick. I focused my mind, let out a yell, and hit the brick with the side of my hand. To my surprise, the brick did not break, and my hand instantly swelled up. I was unable to try it again because of my hand injury.

For a whole week, I was thinking about the brick. My emotions were anger and uncertainty. I then thought of just relaxing and giving my hand time to heal, and I put in my mind that I was going to smash that brick. Each day, I supplied positive thoughts to my mind, like "I will break the brick." I visualized myself breaking the brick. It had been about three weeks since the first attempt. I was now ready to attempt it again. I approached the red brick break with a positive mind. This time. I knew that I would need an extremely powerful strike using my mind, my physical strength, and my spirit. I focused on the brick, thinking through it. I yelled, lifted my hand high in the air, and hit the brick with a perfect strike and *bang*! I split it in half. I did not feel it at all. My focus and mental powers were so strong. It was like breaking a thin board. I then began to understand the power of the mind.

After I became a black belt, I became a full-time karate instructor. This allowed me to practice my martial arts and continue to work on meditation and developing the mind. Over the next eight years, I successfully split several red bricks and cement blocks in karate demonstrations and shows. In those eight years, I practiced meditation and ancient breathing exercises. When I became a master, I began performing more feats of the mind. My next feat was to walk, jump, and lie on jagged, broken glass and not get cut. This feat is performed through the development of a mind-body relationship. Through meditation, you develop an understanding of the body, so in order to perform this feat and not get cut, you must relax your body and become liquid. Although the body has bones, it is 80 percent liquid. So through the meditation, you relax, absorb the sharpness of the glass, and do not get cut.

When I would perform this feat, I would transfer my mind into a state of concentration and not feel any pain. After performing this feat, I continued my meditation and breathing exercises. For my next feat, I took sharpened Harley-Davidson motorcycle spokes, pierced them through my arms, and hung buckets of water from the spokes. Through meditation and concentrated, relaxed breathing, I was able to slow my metabolism down and avoid bleeding. With the spokes in my arms, I would then stand atop razor-sharp samurai swords and have a weight hanging from my teeth. I would perform this feat with no bleeding and no pain. I performed this feat many times around the world on TV and in magazine stories. I am recognized in the *Guinness Book of World Records* for the most amazing feat of mind power called "The Mind Warrior." Having developed the power of the mind I knew that I could always find a way to overcome the impossible. To overcome the impossible, you need the power of your mind, and you need the positive strength derived from the mind.

Chapter 2

Never Accepting Defeat

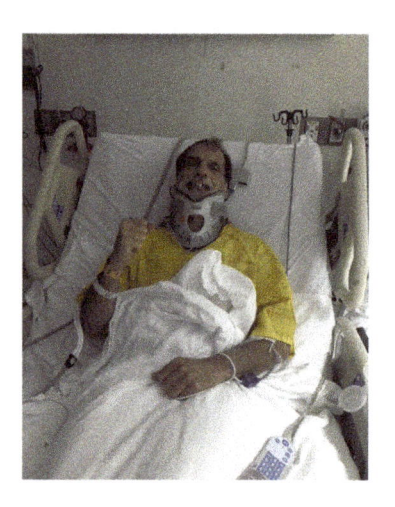

The Hospital

I was admitted to the hospital at eleven in the evening and spent the first night in the emergency room in the intensive care unit. The biggest concern was that I was not allowed to move my neck at all. I had to lie in bed, and I was braced not to move. I was also being checked every hour for signs of a concussion. I was being administered pain medication and intervening liquids. I had a heart monitor on, and my pulse was being metered. I knew I had a serious injury, just in the way that they handled me and the way they were checking me. However, I lay there very uncomfortably. I had so many bruises. Every bone in my body was hurting. The pain medication put my mind in a relaxed state, but my body was still aching and throbbing in different places. Although I lay there strapped down and under so much care, I knew in my heart that I was going to get through this and that I was going to heal completely. I just had that feeling.

The next day, I was moved to a regular room in the hospital. The doctor came in and sat on the edge of my bed. He asked me some questions about the motorcycle and the accident. He then went on to say how lucky I was to be alive, and even luckier not to be paralyzed. He explained about the fracture of C1 and how it was separated and broken in three places. He said I had to be extremely careful not to trip, fall, cough, or sneeze, or the bone could slip, and I would have a stroke. The result of that would be either penalization or death. He explained about the nerves and that they all go through C1. Therefore, it was such a serious injury.

He asked me, "What is your occupation?"

I said, "I am a master of karate, and I teach karate, boxing, and fitness classes."

He went on to say, "Well, you may never be able to do karate again. You have a very serious injury, and you must be very careful. You may be able to do exercises again, but I do not think you will be able to do any contact sports again in your life."

I was shocked that the doctor was so strong, and he sounded like I did not have a chance. I smiled at the doctor and said it with confidence. "I will be fine, doctor." I knew that to conquer this injury, I had to have complete confidence. I had to trust my inner self and never allow defeat. No matter how bad the situation looked, I would never think negatively. That was in my mind, and nothing was going to change it.

The doctor said that I was okay with the concussion and that most of the other injuries would heal in a week or so. He reminded me that I had a very serious accident and that I must take it slow and easy. However, my personality was never slow and easy, but I was going to listen to the doctor and try my hardest to overcome the fractured neck.

As I lay in the hospital bed, I kept thinking that I had to get out of the hospital to heal. I kept thinking that only sick people stay in the hospital, and I needed to get out. I got through the rest of the day and night. I could never sleep more than an hour at a time. The neck brace was so uncomfortable. Imagine having a hard plastic brace wrapped tightly around your neck for twenty-four hours a day. It was hard to talk because it was supported under my chin. When I would fall asleep, I would wake up thinking that I was being chocked. There was also constant throbbing pain on the right side of my neck and down my shoulder.

The next day, the doctor came into my room. I asked the doctor what I had to do to get out of the hospital and what his projection was for when I would get out of the hospital. He said that I would probably have to be in the hospital for ten to fourteen days. He said that I must get past the serious stage, in which I could have a stroke. He said, "We must keep a close eye on your progress and your bone healing. Your nerves have been damaged, which will influence your balance. You will have to do some tests before I can release you. When you can walk in a straight line, one foot in front of another, to show that you have regained your balance, that is the first test. Then you will have to walk up and down a flight of stairs to show me that you have your strength back. I would have to see you walk normally without any wobble or uncertainty in your movements."

I asked the doctor, "Can I get out of bed and practice?" He said yes, but I had to be very careful. He said I can walk around the floor of the hospital but have not taken any steps yet. We shook hands, and I said, "Doctor, I am going to overcome this. I am confident. I will be fine. I promise to be careful, but I cannot just sit here and do nothing." He just smiled and looked at me like I was crazy, but he did not know me. I have so much inner strength, and I am filled with determination. I now wanted to prove to the doctors that I was going to overcome the unbelievable.

After the doctor left, I got out of bed, and I could hardly stand without a wobble. I took a few steps, and then I went out into the hall. I walked a little, and then I would stand for a minute. I was thinking that I could hardly walk; how could I do the step-in front test of putting one foot in front of the other? Well, I walked for about five minutes and went back to my bed. About an hour later, I got out of bed and took a walk. This time, I made a complete revolution around the hospital floor. I went back to my bed and rested. I continued doing laps every hour. Soon, I got up to doing two laps an hour. All the nurses and attendants were surprised by my determination.

The next morning, I tried to do the test of one foot in front of the other, but I could not do it. My balance was very much affected by the accident. I could not tell if it was from the head injury I took or from the damaged nerves in my neck. Every hour, I was on my walk. All the nurses were saying, "You want to get out of here. Don't you?"

I said, "Yes, my goal is to get out tomorrow."

On the fourth day, early in the morning, I tried the step-in front test, and I did it. I then went down the hall to the doors of the steps and walked up and then down the steps. The steps were really challenging. First, I lacked strength, and secondly, balance. When I got to the top, I got a little dizzy, but I just took a deep breath, focused my mind, and gingerly went down. When I got to the bottom, I said, "YES! I am getting out of this place."

At about noon, the doctor came in, and I said, "Doctor, I am ready to take the test and go home."

He checked my vital signs and said, "Okay, let me see you do the test."

I stood up and did the one foot in front of another walk with no wobble.

He then said, "Take a walk up the hall," as he walked behind me. We got to the door of the steps, and he said, "Go ahead and walk up the flight of steps." I walked up and then walked down. He said, "I am impressed. You did it so quickly. I will sign you out today, but remember to be very careful." He recommended Dr. Weiner of Cherry Hill. He said he was the top neck surgeon in the area and that I should make an appointment to see him.

I was excited to get out of the hospital after just four days when the doctors thought I would be in there for a few weeks. I was eager to get to the comforts of my home. On the ride home, I felt every bump on the road. I realized that my body was weak and injured. My next step was to focus my mind and direct my spirit to heal and be strong again. I was not discouraged. I just knew I had a major task to accomplish. I was up against a big tiger. There is an old story in the martial arts about the warrior and the tiger. The warrior trains sincerely for many years, and to become a true warrior, he must one day face and conquer the tiger. When he conquers the tiger, he becomes the tiger. The idea of the story is that, on the path of life, we will all be confronted by a tiger one day. The story tells how the fight between the two went. The tiger was mighty and powerful, but the warrior had a heart, a soul, and the ability to think. After a fierce battle, the warrior wins the fight, and he goes on to become the greatest warrior of all time. On the ride home, I implanted the thought of the tiger, and I was now going to be focused on conquering it.

When I got home, it was nice to be there, but it was not easy. I was now on no medication at all. The doctor gave me a bottle of pain pills, but I never took them. I personally do not like any pain medication. The pain medication slows down healing and weakens your mind and spirit. Plus, I was not interested in taking anything that could be physically addicting. I had to wear my plastic neck brace twenty-four hours a day. I could not lean forward, and I could not lie down. So imagine that you have to wear a very uncomfortable plastic brace tightly around your neck. You are restricted from any exercise or quick movements. You must rest and sleep in a recliner chair, and you cannot drive or put yourself around people in fear of an unintentional bump. With the brace, it was impossible to get a full night of sleep. I would sleep for an hour and then wake up. That was the way my nights went the whole time I was in the brace. The funny part is that when you have no choice in the matter, you get stronger, and you learn to deal with whatever you are faced with. I could not even take the brace off to take a shower. I was also dealing with lots of pain in my neck, ribs, and shoulders. I could hardly lift my right arm. It was so painful. My severely bruised ribs also hurt each time I took a breath, but I felt like I was on the path of recovery.

At home, learning to do the little things again was my first challenge. My strength, balance, and perception were all affected by the damage to the nerves in my neck. Getting up to walk to the kitchen required a lot of effort. First, I had to concentrate on the task, then I would stand, establish my balance, and then do the task slowly with caution and safety in mind. But each time I did it, I was getting stronger and faster. In my house, there is a set of steps going upstairs for the bedrooms and showers. It starts off with three steps turning to the left, then ten steps to the second floor. The first time I had to go up the steps, it was very scary. I had to really concentrate on each step and work my way up. When it was time to go back down, it was harder. Each step was a task of concentration. But each time I went up those steps, I got stronger and felt the progress. All I kept thinking was that I had to keep pushing myself, and I had to keep a strong, positive mind to conquer all these injuries. I was determined to not let this defeat me.

I put into my mind that I would never accept defeat and that I was going to work with my mind and body to completely heal. I was very determined to face the challenge. Deep down inside of me, I knew that I was going to conquer the injury and return to being the same person I was before the injury. My martial arts training gave me the strength to focus my inner self on never quitting and never giving up.

DOMINICK GIACOBBE

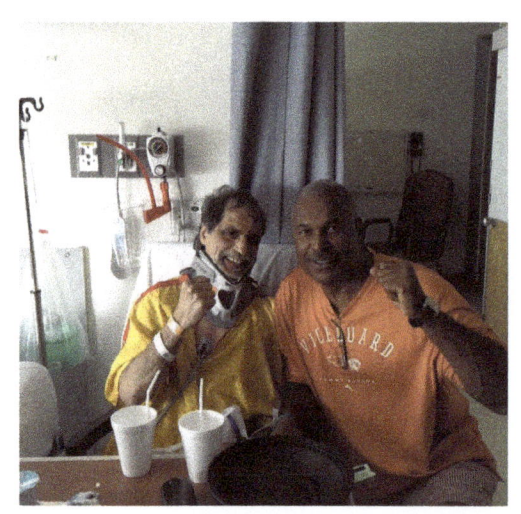

My good friend and former NFL player, Al Chesley,
came to visit me at Cooper Hospital.

What you create in your mind, you create in your life. Create positive images, and you will have positive actions. Create the image of you being a strong, powerful person, and that is what you will be. The power is in your thoughts. (D. A. Giacobbe)

Chapter 3

My Doctor

Dr. Jeffrey Gleimer

The first week at home was very difficult. I had very little sleep. It was also very difficult to eat because all my teeth were injured and loose, and the nerves were all sensitive. I had to eat soft foods and lots of liquids. On my regular work schedule, I would work twelve hours a day, teaching and doing workouts four to five hours a day, and now all I did was rest and try to heal. I had an appointment with the new neck specialist, Dr. Jeffrey Gleimer, a week after I got out of the hospital. I had to bring all my CAT scans and X-rays taken at the hospital. I had to be driven to the doctor's office because I was unable to drive with the brace on my neck. I was still dealing with a lot of pain in my neck and body. I was also still having problems with my shoulder. I could not lift my arm as high as my shoulder. The body pains and aches were not going away. I was wondering if I was ever going to feel good again.

Angie and I arrived at the doctor's office. After a twenty-minute wait, we were brought back to a patient's room. The doctor came, introduced himself to me, and began looking at my reports and scans. He asked me what I did for a living. I told him I was a martial arts instructor, and I owned a karate school and fitness center. He seemed very interested in my martial arts. He asked me a few questions about the arts and said he had practiced some martial arts. He went on to say, "Well, you have a serious situation here, and you may never be able to do martial arts again."

I quickly responded, "Doctor, are you telling me the truth?" My attitude was that I was going to be alright.

He said, "Listen to me. This is no joke. The slightest movement will cause you to have a stroke, and you will either die or be totally paralyzed." He went on to say how lucky I was to be able to walk with a C1 fracture. Although I was hearing all this negative news, in my mind, I was still confident that I was going to be okay. He checked the CAT scan of my shoulder and ribs, and they were just deep bruises and would not need surgery. He said I would have to wear the neck brace for fourteen to twenty weeks.

I said, "What?" I thought he was joking because the doctor in the hospital told me that I would be in the brace for six weeks. I told the doctor that the hospital said I would be in the brace for six weeks.

He said, "Yes, they left the bad news for me." He also said that he might have to operate on my neck to reconnect the bone. He explained how the bone was a circle, and he would go in and put a small pin in the bone, connecting the two pieces again. If he operated, I would then be in the halo brace for another six months. Dr. Gleimer took another look at one of the X-rays and said, "Right now, we will just wait and see how your bones heal." I think he knew that I was not too interested in having an operation. We shook hands, and he said he wanted to see me in two weeks. Before each visit, I had to get a CAT scan so he could see any progress. I was so discouraged, thinking that there was no way that I could wear this brace for another fourteen weeks. That was impossible. I was thinking, *What a torture it would be.*

He also said, "Do not remove the brace. It must be twenty-four hours a day. He went on to explain to me that I had the same break as Christopher Reeves, who was totally paralyzed. Reeves broke C1, falling off a horse, and he never walked again. He instructed me to be very careful. He said, "Take your time and go slowly." I asked him if I could do tai chi and chi gong. He smiled and said, "Yes, you can. Do it very slowly, and if you feel any pain, stop immediately." He studied martial arts himself, and he knew that the art of tai chi would help me heal. As I was leaving the office, I told the doctor that I would be 100 percent healed from this injury. He saw my confidence and seemed nervous that I might do something to hurt myself, but I was not going to take any chances. I just knew from reading my body how I was getting better each day. I knew I was going to heal.

The next day, I began doing my tai chi moves mostly in place, and I also did my chi gong. This became a daily routine, working on my moves. I also began doing light exercises and just moving my arms and legs. Within a few days, I was beginning to feel stronger. I then began doing lunges and squats just to strengthen my legs. When I did the exercises, I paid close attention to my neck, keeping it erect and straight. If I felt any pain, I would stop, relax, take a few breaths, and start again. I was doing everything slowly and carefully. Although the doctor was telling me all the negatives, I had a positive mind, and I kept saying to myself that I would conquer this injury. I knew I did not want the operation to reconnect the bone. I felt that if I had an operation, I would never be the same again. I had to develop a plan of recovery, so I began doing research on the computer about fractures and about healing bones. I was determined to make a plan to conquer this obstacle I was faced with. I wanted to prove to the doctor that I would be his biggest success story that he ever dealt with. He was the doctor, and I was the injured patient, but I would not allow the injury to discourage me anyway. Still, I was dealing with all the challenges and the facts, but I would not allow any of that to stop my positive mindset.

Moving forward, I would have to visit the doctor every two weeks. Before each visit, I had to get a CAT scan at least three days before, and at every other visit, I had to get an MRI. Going through these X-rays, scans, and MRIs was very difficult. Remember, I was in a neck brace, unable to lie down. These tests would have to be done with the brace on, so sometimes it took several tries to get it right. I was realizing that nothing was easy with a broken neck. Dr. Gleimer and I became friends.

We spoke often, and he was very encouraging. I believe he hesitated on the operation because he wanted to see if I could heal myself. Each time I visited, there was some positive news about my healing.

About six weeks after the accident, two of my students from Belgium, Master Stephanie Huguier and Pieter Rubens, came to the USA and took me to a baseball game. I refused to stay at home and be a vegetable.

The will is stronger than the sword. The internal feeds the external. The will and determination to succeed will always lead to success and victory. (D. A. Giacobbe)

Chapter 4

Making the Plan

Making a plan of attack was the next focus of my thoughts. I had to figure out how I could heal my fractured neck and go back to being the same person I was before the accident. I figured I would do the tai chi and chi gong to create healing chi to correct the damage to the meridians in the injured area. The chi would also help in the healing of the bones and nerves. I figured that I would go on a very strict low-fat diet, consuming lots of collagen, protein, and vitamins. I decided to add lower body exercise to the program, using the concept that the body is a whole, and if I make my legs stronger, my whole body will get stronger. I figured I would do a shoulder and trapezoid muscle routine to strengthen the supporting muscles of the neck. I also decided to do the special breathing exercises from my *Tang Soo Do* training to increase the strength of my internal spirit.

In the art of *Tang Soo Do*, we have special deep breathing exercises that date back hundreds of years. These exercises are designed to increase the flow of oxygen to the blood, which promotes eternal healing. There are four basic breathing exercises, which were taught to me many years ago when I traveled to Korea in the '70s for special training. We would do these exercises before performing feats of the mind. We also performed some of the breathing exercises before breaking boards or cement blocks. The other benefits of deep breathing are that it forces huge amounts of oxygen into the blood and increases the lungs' capacity to absorb large amounts of oxygen into the brain. These are known to strengthen the body and prevent aging, and they also aid in bone and organ strength. There are four breathing exercises, which I perform at least five days a week. The four breathing exercises are the bear, eagle, tiger, and wild boar. I was also taught that by performing these exercises on a regular basis, it would have a major effect on slowing down the aging of the brain and would keep the blood vessels of the body young and strong. Oxygen is food for the brain, and the more you can supply it to the brain, the longer it will last. I also felt that the breathing exercises would aid in the healing of my neck because more oxygen to the blood would promote stronger bones and would also help with bone density.

Next is a complete explanation of the ancient breathing exercises, which I performed on a regular basis. The four exercises are simple and contribute to good health and a long life.

The Bear

Begin with your legs spread apart, your feet flat on the ground, and your knees slightly bent. Place your hands in front of your groin area, with your first finger and thumb touching each other and forming a triangle. Move your arms up quickly above your head. On the way up, take a strong and powerful inhale. When your hands reach above your head, begin to open your hands in a circular fashion, bringing your hands to the side of your chest. From the point when you begin to open your arms, hold your breath, forcing oxygen into your lungs. Do the opening part of the exercise slowly. Then powerfully push your hands downward to the same position as you began the exercise and let out a powerful exhale, pushing all the oxygen out of your lungs. Without waiting, perform the exercise again. Do this exercise at least ten times in a row. In the beginning, you may feel dizzy from the increased flow of oxygen to your brain, but this is okay.

The Eagle

Keeping your legs in the same position, this time start with your hands in front of your body about solar plexus level as if you are holding a volleyball. Next, open your arms as wide as you can, as if an eagle were spreading its wings. As you open your arms, take a powerful inhale. When you reach the open position, hold your breath for two or three seconds, then give a powerful exhale, returning your hands to the starting position. When you are in the open position, expand your chest as much as possible. Repeat this exercise ten times.

The Tiger

Start this exercise with the legs in the same position. Place your hands in front of your groin. Place your left hand on top of your right hand. Next, bring your arms straight up above your shoulders, high above your head, as a tiger raises its paws before leaping to attack its prey. As in the other exercises, take a powerful inhale as you move your hands up. When you reach the top position, hold your breath for two to three seconds. Be sure to expand your chest as much as possible when lifting your arms. Next, return your hands to their original positions, letting out a powerful exhale. Perform this exercise ten times in a row, forcing as much oxygen into your lungs with each inhale.

The Wild Boar

This time, stand straight with feet as wide as your shoulders. Place both hands on your stomach. This is a reverse breathing exercise. When you inhale, force your stomach out, and when you exhale, suck your stomach in. Imagine how the wild boar breathes—quick and powerfully fast in and out breaths. Now do this exercise ten times quickly without stopping. Take in quick, powerful inhales and push out powerful exhales.

These are very good exercises to enhance your health and help in the flow of blood into your brain and organs. I believe that these exercises were a very important factor in the healing of my neck.

The first part of my plan was to start with the tai chi and chi gong exercises because these movements were done slowly and easily. I could exercise without any risk to my neck. I did the movements once or twice a day for about ten minutes. As I did the exercises, the pain in my neck was beginning to relieve. I was also getting stronger. After a few weeks of just doing the chi exercises, I was ready to increase my program.

I was now into week four after the accident. At this point, my shoulder had made very strong progress. Most of the pain was out, and I had about 80 percent of my movements back. My ribs also made a big improvement, but if I took a deep breath, I would still feel it. My ability to walk was stronger and more comfortable. I was on the road to healing.

Next, I began with my tai chi movements not standing in one place. I felt very clumsy and uncoordinated. Going through the moves with the neck brace on was also distracting. After about twenty minutes of doing tai chi, I took a rest. I then did my chi gong exercises for another twenty minutes. The chi exercises were very soft and fluent and required no strength. After I completed all my routines, I stood there, closed my eyes, and meditated on relaxing and allowing my chi energy to flow through my body. I could feel the chi flowing in my body because I just completed the tai chi and chi gong training.

Later that day, I worked out a shoulder-and-trapezoid exercise pattern. I used no weights but did five sets of ten reps for each exercise. For example, I did shoulder shrugs, ten straight up, ten rolling forward, and ten rolling backward. I did those ten times for five sets. I made ten different exercises and did five sets of each. This would be important to strengthen the muscles closest to the injury.

I laid out a leg routine to build and strengthen the larger muscles of the body. Knowing that the stronger the large muscles are, the stronger the body is.

This was my routine, all done with no weights.

> ten squats five times
> ten front lunges five times
> ten wide squats five times
> ten back lunges five times
> ten side-to-side lunges five times
> fifty toe raisers
> twenty step-ups on a small box

Step-ups are done by putting one foot on the box, taking the other foot, and stepping up and down. Use the same leg twenty times, then change legs and do another twenty. I would have to do this exercise very gently, restricting any bouncing. But I did understand the body, and I knew that slight bouncing would enhance bone growth. I had to walk a fine line. You need to push yourself, but you cannot go too hard to damage your progress.

This routine was very exhausting, especially after not exercising for three weeks. However, I knew that hard exercise would increase my strength and balance and aid in bone strength. When the bones are healthy and strong, the body will also be healthy and strong.

I then began my deep breathing exercise routine on a regular basis. These exercises were making me stronger. They were also increasing the lungs' ability to take in more oxygen. The more oxygen in the body, the better the blood flows, and more oxygen supplied to the brain will promote health and healing. Also, large amounts of oxygen in the blood will enhance the healing of nerves and muscles. Deep breathing also increases your energy level. These exercises promote internal strength.

My final routine was meditation. I would do it at night, sitting in the recliner chair, before going to sleep. I would meditate on my body to go into a deep state of relaxation. I would then meditate on my body to heal my neck. I was a student of meditation for many years, and I understood the benefits of meditation. There are many amazing accomplishments obtained through the power of meditation and positive thinking. In the past few years, I have performed many feats of mind over matter. I truly understood and believed in the power of the mind and the internal spirit. The internal spirit can overcome the physical.

Meditation is done by relaxing your body and clearing your mind of all thoughts. The monks say meditation sweeps away the worldly dust. To meditate, you must find a peaceful, calm area where you will not be disturbed or bothered. Simply close your eyes and relax your body. Create a sound or a number and repeat it on each exhale. At first, it may feel like you are not getting any results, but if you keep trying, you will soon feel the relaxation and peace in your mind. I often tell the students to repeat the number one and try to visualize the number in their minds. When you get to the place where no thoughts enter your mind, take out the number, and you will then be contracting with nothingness. This is the type of meditation the Tibetan monks do. I would meditate for about twenty minutes a day, four or five times a week. There is one thing to remember when doing meditation. Quality is more important than quantity.

I then had my routine, and I figured I would do the physical exercises several times a week. Since I had developed the plan, I would need the discipline and determination to stick with it. I knew that my routine would help me make a successful recovery. I was confident that if I did everything as planned, I would be able to overcome my fractured neck.

Planning or setting a goal is very important to finding success. My many years of studying martial arts gave me a lot of knowledge about the body and mind, and I now had to put these many years of experience into practice. My goal was to eliminate the pain, be stronger, and completely heal. I was very determined to not just heal but to be able to practice martial arts the same as I did before the accident. I was also focused on not living a life of pain. So my goal was to completely heal and be the same person as I was before the accident.

> The wise man thinks before he acts, but he will not procrastinate.
> The strong man stands tall when he faces his enemy, but
> he will not retreat out of fear. To be wise and to be strong
> are the greatest qualities for success. (D. A. Giacobbe)

Chapter 5

The Road to Recovery

I knew my road to recovery was not going to be easy. Dealing with a very uncomfortable neck brace for twenty-four hours a day was a major hurdle to get over. You could never get used to wearing it. Everything you did was affected by your neck movement, and not being able to turn from side to side was difficult to deal with. Also, not being able to tilt your head down means you cannot see your feet when walking. These were the inconvenient challenges that I had no control over. However, the major challenge was to heal the bones in my neck and to get them to grow together so I could be a full martial artist again, which was the big picture.

After about two weeks, most of my muscle aches and bruises healed. However, I still had issues with sleeping. Wearing a neck brace twenty-four hours a day was extremely difficult. Each day, the mental aspect of being in that brace got worse. It took a lot to stop myself from just ripping it off. My teeth were another major issue that I had to deal with. One of my teachers, Grand Master Jin Lu of China, taught me about Chinese traditional medicine. He taught me an old technique of tap therapy to send chi to an area for healing. Since my teeth were all weak, I decided to try it with my teeth. I tapped my teeth together a couple of hundred times a day, and sure enough, they began to tighten up. Just after the accident, I visited a dental surgeon. He looked at my teeth and told me that my situation was very bad, and I would probably lose all of them. In most adults, once a tooth is knocked loose, it rarely ever tightens back up again.

Into the fifth week, I was on my daily routine of exercise and meditation. I sent for some special products of protein and collagen. I would make a fruit smoothie every morning and put the vital proteins into the mix. I also took vitamin pills filled with collagen and other essential ingredients for muscle and bone growth. My energy level was very high, and my balance was getting back to normal. Walking was normal again. My teeth began to make improvements. The back teeth firmed up, so I was now able to eat solid foods with my back teeth. I was still unable to bite a sandwich or bread of any kind. The front teeth were still loose.

That week, I went for another CAT scan. I would have to get a CAT scan before each of my doctor's visits. He would have to analyze and compare one scan to the other to see any changes or developments. Getting the CAT scan was never easy. I was unable to lie down, so they always had to work hard to figure out how it could be done. They also had to work around the neck brace. I got the CAT scan, and they told me to come back in two days to get the CD for the doctor.

The next week, I visited my doctor again. He looked at my CAT scan and said that everything was looking good. He said the back of my neck, where the thick bone is, had one hundred hairline fractures, but they were starting to calcify and grow back into a solid bone. That was good news. I said, "Does that mean I can get my brace off sooner?"

He said, "No way." He went on to remind me that I had a very bad break, and it needed time to heal. Until the bones grew back together again, I was at high risk of getting a stroke. He said, "Again, I do not think you will ever be able to do all the things you did before in martial arts. You will probably never be able to punch or kick a heavy bag, and as far as sparring, that will be forbidden. Jumping and snapping movements will also be out of the question." I would respond to the doctor that I was going to be okay and that I would eventually be back to doing everything. I would always show my confidence and positive attitude. I think sometimes he would think that I was crazy. He would also say that if those bones did not grow together, I still might need the operation. I knew I did not want an operation, and I would tell the doctor that I would not need the operation.

OVERCOME

Now that I was feeling better, I began going to my karate school, the Tang Soo Karate and Boxing Academy, which was my place of business. I felt that I would benefit better by being at school rather than being home doing nothing. So I had put that into my routine. I would go to the school every day, watch classes, and give advice to the instructors. Being at the karate school gave me a stronger attitude and motivated me to work harder on my physical conditioning. I was determined to have no setbacks, so I always worked with extreme caution.

The next week, I went to the dentist to have my teeth worked on. The top left tooth was knocked out, and the bottom front teeth were all still loose. The one lower tooth was very loose. The dentist had to work around my neck brace, and I could not lean back, so it was not easy to work on me. They did a set of X-rays, and the dentist looked them over. He said that the one lower front tooth broke below the gum, and he would have to get that out as soon as possible because it would become infected, and I could lose the entire group of five teeth, which were all still a little loose.

I said to the dentist, "Okay, go ahead and remove it." Within the next hour, the tooth was gone, and I now had two front teeth missing—one on the top and one on the bottom. With the bottom tooth out, it was causing me to whistle when I would pronounce certain words. After getting that tooth out in the next few days, the lower teeth made many improvements, and they were all getting tighter and feeling better.

Being a student of *Tang Soo Do*, the art of Korean karate, for forty-eight years at the time of my injury, I had a very strong belief in overcoming the supernatural and the unbelievable. As a *Tang Soo Do* student, you believe you can conquer any feat you are faced with. Being at school reinforced that inner strength and inner confidence. I knew I had the strength, discipline, and determination to overcome the injury. I was now getting power from the spirit of the academy. In *Tang Soo Do*, we say that to get the full potential out of ourselves, we must display mind, body, and spirit. I would always consult my inner philosophy and spiritual self to find answers to my questions.

My teacher would say to me that all the answers to your health are within your inner self. Meditation develops communication between your mind and inner self. So if you are in tune with your inner self, you can find the path to success. I knew my direction. I just had to keep being positive and strong and keep pushing myself to overcome the roadblock I was faced with.

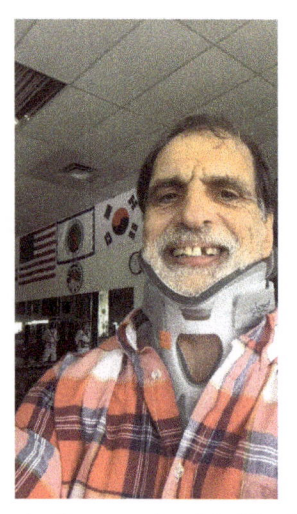

This was at the karate school in Voorhees, New Jersey, while recovering from the accident.

I continued for another two weeks. Everything was making improvements. My body was feeling stronger, and my routines were keeping me positive. I was still not able to sleep for more than an hour at a time with the neck brace on. I would sleep for an hour, get up for thirty minutes, then go back to sleep for another hour. Through this whole ordeal, I was always tired and sleep-deprived.

Again, I had to take another CAT scan and visit my doctor. This time, the doctor said that the back part healed very nicely, the bone was completely calcified, and it showed nice improvement. The side of the neck where I had a fracture also showed considerable healing, but the right side was still separated. He showed me the picture and explained where the bone was and where it was supposed to be. I could see in the scan the separation. He said, "Until that comes back together, you are at risk of a stroke." He said we still must wait and see how it will heal. I was a little discouraged because I wanted all the good news, and I wanted to hear that it made amazing advancements, but I was still in the danger zone. However, although I was a little upset, it still did not stop me from thinking that I was on the path to conquering this.

Another two weeks passed, and I was back at the doctor's office with my CAT scan. This time, he said again that everything was healing except the separation. He said that he might have to operate and put a pin in the bone to help it grow together. I knew that if I were to get an operation, my martial arts future would be over. I told the doctor that I didn't want an operation. He said he didn't want to do an operation either, but it might be what he had to do if the bone did not heal. He kept looking at all the different CAT scans and said that maybe we should get another opinion. He said the best neck doctor in the Philadelphia area was the head doctor at Jefferson Hospital in Philadelphia. He said he would contact him and set up an appointment for me to go see him. I really respected my doctor for doing that. My doctor was a younger doctor in his forties, and he was going to send me to an older and more experienced doctor. That was a very honorable thing for my doctor to do. He was so concerned about my future that he humbled himself to send me to one of the top spine doctors in the country. I had a lot of respect for my doctor anyway. He was very smart and explained everything so clearly. He had so much knowledge about the body, especially the spine.

The next day, I got a call from the Jefferson Hospital in Philadelphia. The lady told me that she was the doctor's nurse and that I had an appointment in five days. She went on to tell me to take two regular full-strength aspirins every day from now until my appointment. I said, "Okay," but to myself, I was thinking, *Why would I have to take aspirins?* Well, I then figured that it was going to be for some sort of test. I continued working every day. I kept myself very busy, although I was very limited physically.

The day finally arrived; it was the day to meet the special spine doctor from Jefferson. I was excited to see what he was going to say. When I got to the office, there were several patients in wheelchairs who were paralyzed. It was a scary site. I understood that this is the effect of most people who break their necks. I thought about how I was so blessed to be able to walk. I sat in the lobby with all my CAT scans and X-rays. They called me in, and the nurse checked my blood pressure and did a few tests. Next, the doctor came in and looked at me. He then put all the CAT scans on a big TV screen and began comparing them. He did a few tests with my arms and said that he agreed with my doctor that I was making strong progress and that he did not think an operation would be necessary at this time. It was good news and gave me a strong feeling of hope. Before the doctor left, I asked him, "Why did you have me take aspirin before this visit?"

He responded, "Well, I saw your age and your first CAT scan, and with my knowledge of spines, I thought you were a strong candidate for a stroke. But now, after seeing you and seeing your strength, I see that you are very healthy and not at risk of getting a stroke."

I said, "I could have told you that, doctor." He smiled. I saw more doctors in two months than I had in my entire life. I was learning so much about the body and how it functions. I enjoyed listening to them talk in doctor talk. I tried to put every part of my ordeal in a positive direction.

The next week, I had to go back to my doctor, and this time, he wanted me to get a CAT scan and MRI. The CAT scan was okay, but the MRI was a big problem. At the imagining office, the lady said that I had to take the neck brace off and lay in the tube. I said, "I am sorry, but my doctor said I cannot take the brace off." She went on to say that she does this all the time and that she cannot do the MRI with the brace on. So I said, "Forget the MRI. I have to talk to my doctor before I do it." One thing for sure was that I was not taking any chances with my neck.

When I went to my doctor, he said, "I see you have the CAT scan. What about the MRI?"

I said, "The lady wanted me to take off the brace and lay in the tube. I said no. I could not take the brace off."

His face turned red, and he said, "I am happy that you listened to me. I put a note on the script not to take your brace off." He went right to the phone and called the place and gave them a piece of his mind. He gave me another script and wrote a big "Do not take the brace off." After we got through that, he went on to say that the doctor from Jefferson agreed with him and felt that I was making very good progress and should not need an operation at this time. He also said that I should be able to do martial arts again, but with limited action. Like no sparring, no hitting bags, no breaking boards, and no jumping.

I said sarcastically, "Wow, doc! What is left?"

He said, "You will be at risk of a stroke for the rest of your life. Remember, if that bone slips, you're done. You will have to be careful of any jolting action on your body for the rest of your life."

I said, "Do not worry, sir. I will be back 100 percent. I am confident." As usual, he would just smile at me and shake his head.

I was thinking of the amazing support system I was surrounded by. So many people were helping me in so many ways. My girlfriend, Angela Mastrando, had to drive me everywhere, and she helped with the brace for cleaning and taking care of me on a daily routine. My daughter, Kimberly Giacobbe Barsky, was by my side throughout the whole experience. She took care of all the business at the academy. My sister, Barbara Giacobbe, helped with teaching all the karate classes at the school. I had a constant flow of calls every day. When I was in the hospital, I got a call from my karate teacher, Grand Master Chun Sik Kim. He was the teacher who made me a black belt and who taught me how to be an instructor. He was so worried about me. But hearing his voice and his words of encouragement meant a lot to me. He gave me the powerful energy I needed. One of my other teachers and a highly respected martial artist, Grand Master Ki Yun Yi, called me and gave me kind words of wisdom and encouragement. Master Don Straga was up to see me and called me every day. Master Keith Bennett, my student and true Tang Soo Brother, drove for four hours to see me in the hospital and sat there with me for two hours, then drove back. He called me every day and wanted to know my progress. When you are faced with a major injury and the downside is much stronger than the upside, the encouragement you get from everyone is what gives you the strength to conquer the battle.

I also realized the divine or spiritual side of surviving my accident, getting a broken neck, and still being alive. I feel a closer bond with the spiritual aspects of my life now. I truly believe that God, an angel, or a spirit was with me and gave me the strength and power to survive. I was now tapping into that spiritual power, making it work to completely heal me. I said many prayers and asked for God's help to heal me. I did have this very good feeling that God was hearing my prayers and that healing was in progress. I think that when a human is faced with tragedy, they learn to accept God into their life and into their heart. When you get scared and feel helpless, you look for God's help. I believe God works in strange ways. He may be with you, but you will never get a free ride. He only gives you the opportunity or the direction to help yourself. I also had a picture of Padre Pio at the side of my bed. He was a modern-day saint from Italy. It is known that his presence has healed many people. On one of my visits to Italy in the '90s, I went to Padre Pio's church, and I was amazed. At the altar of the church was the tomb of the saint. I felt the energy coming from the tomb. My fingers were tingling. Hundreds of people were there from all over the world for healing. Many of the people who were sick were healed by his spirit. So when I needed extra help for my healing, I prayed, focused on his picture, and said a prayer. I did this every morning and every night.

The next week, I returned to my doctor. This time, I had another CAT scan and an MRI. Getting the MRI was horrible. They had to put pillows around my head to keep me from moving. I had to lie down, which was very uncomfortable and awkward. However, I relaxed my mind and body and got through it. Lying in the MRI tunnel for forty minutes with a neck brace and pillows all around you is no fun. The doctor looked at the MRI and said, "Well, you fractured your neck in three places. You also herniated C2, and 5 and 6 are bulging. You are a very lucky man. There are not many people in this world who would be walking after fracturing C1 in three places, having C2 herniated, C3 and C4 fractured, and 5 and 6 bulging. That is a very serious neck issue." Although my neck had a serious injury, I was feeling stronger, and I was getting more confident that I was going to completely heal. I had this inner feeling that gave me such a strong feeling of confidence.

It was now mid-November. I had been in a neck brace for fourteen weeks. At this point, I was suffering from lower back pain. My back was hurting so bad from sitting in a recliner and not lying down. I felt pain going down my right leg. Today I was going to see my doctor, and as usual, I had my most recent CAT scan for the visit. I got into the office, and he looked at the scans. He said, "How do you feel?"

I said, "I'm okay. I just have a lot of back pain." He told me to stand and face him. He reached for my neck brace and took it off. It was an overwhelming feeling of weakness and fright.

He said, "Now turn your head slowly to the right." I could not turn much at all. I had to turn my whole body. My neck was stiff as a board. He said, "Turn to the left." It was the same—very stiff. He then said, "Look down." I could not move my neck more than an inch. He said that I am done with the brace and that movement should help it do the final healing. He showed me neck-stretching exercises and said that I had to do them every day. He told me that I was still restricted from jolting movements, no running, and no jumping at all. He showed me the CAT scan of C1, and he showed me how the bone was healing on one side, and on the other side, the bone was still separated. I would have to take it easy until either the bone made a complete bond or if I had a pin inserted.

He ordered me this special electronic stimulator to help with bone growth. I was told by the doctor to wear the stimulator for four hours a day for at least four months. The doctor again said, "Please take it slow and give your neck a chance to heal."

I asked, "Can I lie down now when I go to sleep?" He said yes. I was so happy. The doctor said that for one week, I had to wear the brace every time I was in a car for safety. That meant at least another week of no driving. The doctor told me that he wanted to see me in three months. He recommended physical therapy, but I told him that I was going to do my own therapy. He knew of my experience in karate, tai chi, and fitness, and he felt that I was qualified to do my own therapy.

I said, "Okay, see you in three months." I walked out of the office slowly and was kind of weak and had the feeling of being unprotected, but the feeling of freedom was overwhelming. My new goal was to work my tail off to get the bone to completely heal. I was on a new mission.

> Powerful positive thoughts will make you strong to face your daily battles. Face your challenges and conquer them. The power is in your mind. Powerful thoughts mean positive results. (D. A. Giacobbe)

Chapter 6

Treatment for Success

I was now out of the brace after fourteen horrible weeks. I felt like doing a dance, but I knew that was out of the question. My mind was spinning with what I was going to do to get my neck healed. I started thinking about the CAT scan and how the bone was on the side and that it needed to adjust and move back in alignment so I could have complete success. I figured out a new line of attack. I now had to work on stretching the neck muscles and getting the surrounding muscles strong again. I began each day with neck-stretching exercises. The neck-stretching exercises would be to first look down, trying to get your chin to your chest, then look all the way up, stretching your neck all the way back. Next was each side, first right then left, and last was to stretch side to side, trying to bring your ear to your shoulder. When I first began, my chin was about three inches from my chest, and I would have to work hard to get the muscles to stretch enough to get my chin to my chest. Going side by side was a joke. To look to the side, I had to turn my whole body. Because of the extreme stiffness, I was still unable to drive because I could not turn my head from side to side. At this point, I did not have much pain, only stiffness.

The next thing I did was visual meditation on the bone in my neck, adjusting and moving it into the proper place, and bonding. I did this visual meditation five times a week for twenty minutes each session. When you meditate, your goal is to clear your mind of all thoughts, relax the entire body, and go into a state of nothingness. Most meditations start with a mantra. A mantra is a word or sound repeated to aid concentration in meditation. You focus all your thoughts on the mantra. It then clears your mind of all other thoughts. Being a student of meditation for over forty-five years allowed me to understand how I was going to use the meditation as a healing tool. So now, when I sat down to meditate, I would close my eyes, and instead of using a mantra, I would visualize the CAT scan and the position of the bones. I would then clear my mind and focus on the energy going to that spot and adjusting it to its natural position. I would visualize the bones reconnecting in the correct position. I would breathe very softly, relaxing my entire body, and I would have a great feeling of relaxation. After each session, I would sit and relax for a few minutes and let the energy flow through my body.

I also wore the bone stimulator four hours a day. Wearing the stimulator four hours a day was kind of hard. I could not wear it out in public because if I encountered a person with a heart monitor or a heart pacemaker, it could affect them in a negative way. The stimulator was very uncomfortable, and after an hour, it would start to bother you, but I did it every day. The good thing was that I didn't have to do it four hours in a row. I was able to do it for a total of four hours a day.

Every day, I also did a weightlifting therapy workout, concentrating on my shoulders and surrounding neck muscles. In the past, I had had some shoulder injuries and knew all the shoulder exercises for the shoulders, so I was confident that those exercises would help with the neck. I began with three-pound weights, doing the exercises slowly and carefully. I continued my tai chi and the chi gong three times a week, and I was now back teaching my karate class. The karate class was very motivating. Teaching karate was making me mentally strong. I had a difficult time trying to do my kicks. Doing kicks while concentrating on keeping your head straight took away your natural and fluent movement. I was determined to get better and get my natural karate movements back to the way they were in the past.

The next week, I was able to drive, and everything was improving slowly. All the pain in my neck was gone, and my back also healed from being able to lie down and stretch my leg muscles. About four weeks into my special training program, I was now lifting ten pounds on each dumbbell, and my strength was returning. My neck was turning from side to side much better, and my chin was about an inch from my chest. I still wore the stimulator four hours a day. In my meditation sessions, I would picture my neck, and I would imagine the bone moving into place. I thought of it as a rocking chair, and each time the chair rocked, it moved slightly closer to where it needed to be. I was now getting stronger, and all the pain and stiffness were gone. I knew I still had a lot of work to do to get the muscle strength and flexibility back to normal.

I was now doing tai chi and chi gong five times a week for an hour each session. When doing tai chi and chi gong, you strengthen your inner spirit and chi energy. The concept of acupuncture is that you place a needle on a spot, and it sends healing chi to the injured area. The concept of tai chi and chi gong is to enhance your total chi energy and allow it to flow freely to have a healing effect on any injuries in your body. I felt that doing all these combinations of different concepts was the best avenue for success. I was very determined to beat this challenge I was facing. The one thing I did have from all the years of my *Tang Soo Do* martial arts training was a strong, positive mind. I could honestly say that I was never in a negative state of mind. I wanted victory, and I was determined to find it.

My meditation sessions were getting better and better. I was feeling such a powerful and rewarding feeling from each session. The visual part was helping to concentrate my energy on my neck area. I was feeling more relaxed and calmer during my meditation sessions. The visual part was becoming clearer, and I was feeling the power of the spirit in my neck.

I also began a special chi breathing exercise in which you inhale energy through your nose and send the energy down to your stomach, under your groin, up your back, and to your neck. Hold your breath for twenty seconds and exhale the energy from your neck back down your spine, around your groin, and out of your mouth. This is a breathing technique that sends healing chi to the injured area and releases the injured chi out of your body. I did this breathing exercise ten times a day. I was very determined to use all the different types of healing I learned over the many years of martial arts training.

Now into the third month of lifting, I was now using twenty-pound dumbbells, and I was doing double the workout. The strength was returning, and my muscles were beginning to grow. I did the same routines every day, focusing on healing. My chin was now down to my chest, and I was now able to turn my neck a complete ninety degrees to the right and to the left. I was also able to look up. Looking up was the most difficult to accomplish because it was twice as tight as the other directions of my neck movement.

I was anxious to start running, but until I saw the doctor, I was instructed to stop running. In my workouts, I would walk instead of run. I was also teaching my regular karate classes every day. Although I was teaching, I was instructed by my doctor not to have any contact and no jumping at all. Doing the blocks with my hands was okay, but doing kicks was still a bit difficult. I was now kicking, trying to keep my head in a straight position. I was losing the feeling of the natural kick motion. I was doing all the techniques, but gingerly and without the snapping motion. When doing karate kicks, you thrust them out, and your head and neck snap in a natural way. However, I could not do that because of my neck problem, so my kicks were different. I also noticed that my flexibility was reduced due to injuring the nerves. It affects the tightness in your entire body.

I was also focused on the nutritional aspect of healing. Eating a healthy, low-fat diet was my target. I consumed lots of proteins for bone and muscle growth. No bad foods like sugars and high-fat foods. These all take away your body's ability to heal. I continued to take collagen, which was very important for bone growth. I took a collagen powder mixed in a fresh fruit smoothie drink every morning and two capsules a day with high amounts of natural collagen. Eating healthy is important for the body to regain its natural strength and helps the body heal faster.

The good thing was that, since my job as a karate instructor and fitness coach, I was able to concentrate my entire days on working on healing my body. Although I was doing so much, there was no guarantee that what I was doing would help at all. I just knew that I had to give it 100 percent of my focus and see if I could overcome the odds. Deep down inside, I knew that I was going to conquer this and be back to 100 percent of myself before the accident. I never allowed negativity to overtake my positive direction.

After three months of intense training and therapy, it was time to visit my doctor again. As in the past, I was back at the imaging office, getting another CAT scan. I got the CAT scan a few days before my visit and then went to see the doctor. He took the CAT scan and put it on his computer. He kept looking at it very intensely. I was wondering why he was looking at it for such a long time. He then pulled out my first CAT scan and loaded them both together. He kept looking at them. He stood up and said to me, "You beat the odds."

I said. "What?"

He responded, "I am very impressed that your neck has completely healed. I have never seen that happen before. I do not know what you did, but the bone moved back to its original position and completely healed. You have a green light to do everything you did in the past, which includes jumping, running, and sparring." I was so happy, but deep down inside, I knew that I was going to conquer this. He took pictures of the two CAT scans and said he was sending them to the medical journal. He kept saying, "This never happens. Whatever you did, it worked."

I told the doctor, "You do not want to know what I did," with a big smile. He was so happy, and so was I.

He said, "You are a very lucky man. Most people would have been in a wheelchair for the rest of their lives with a fracture as you had."

I was so happy that I felt like letting out a yell. I kept thinking, *I did it*. Although the bone was healed and I got the green light to resume all my training, I still had a long way to go to get back to the same physical condition as I was in seven months before. But, at least, the danger of being paralyzed was gone forever.

When Angela and I left the office, she gave me a big hug and said, "You did it." I thanked her for all her support and help through this long journey. Although the bone was healed, I still had issues with my balance and flexibility. I was happy, and I appreciated all my martial arts instructors for instilling a martial arts attitude of never retreating in battle.

> Overcome the odds, make it to the top of the mountain, and go beyond your expectations. Go through life with the determination to succeed. When one step is completed, be ready to take the next. (D. A. Giacobbe)

The Study

The Study by a Professor and Surgeons

About four years after my injury, a man joined my karate academy. His name was Gary. At the end of one of my classes, I spoke to the students about overcoming things you may be faced with. I told the students about my injury and how I overcame it. He was fascinated by the story. After the class, he told me that he was a professor and would be interested in doing a study on me. He said he would get all my records and do a complete study. I said, "That would be great."

A study was performed by Dr. Gary Goldberg about my injury—the healing and the unbelievable results. Dr. Goldberg received all the reports, images, and studies done on me during my treatment for the fractured neck. The study was done with several physicians, surgeons, and professors. The name used in the study was Nicholas Giovanni.

Dr. Gary Goldberg

Dr. Goldberg is an associate professor at Rowan University. He has worked at major institutes around the world to elucidate fundamental mechanisms that control cell behavior and develop approaches to understand and combat cancer. His research has been published in over seventy articles that have been referenced thousands of times, a textbook, and several book chapters. He has invented technology described in several issued patents, has presented at numerous national and international meetings, and has run several workshops around the world. He has also founded the pharmaceutical company Sentrimed, the international group PDPN Central to support academic and translational research, and the PBLMed platform to guide medical education. Dr. Goldberg is investigating how growth factor receptors promote tumor cell growth and motility and developing ways to target these receptors to prevent and combat cancer. His work has led to the generation of compounds supported by the NIH and other agencies with IRB and FDA IND approval for clinical trials aimed at preventing and treating cancer. Dr. Goldberg is working with colleagues at research centers in the USA and other countries to develop these compounds into pharmaceutical reagents that can be used to treat cancer as well as inflammatory diseases, including arthritis.

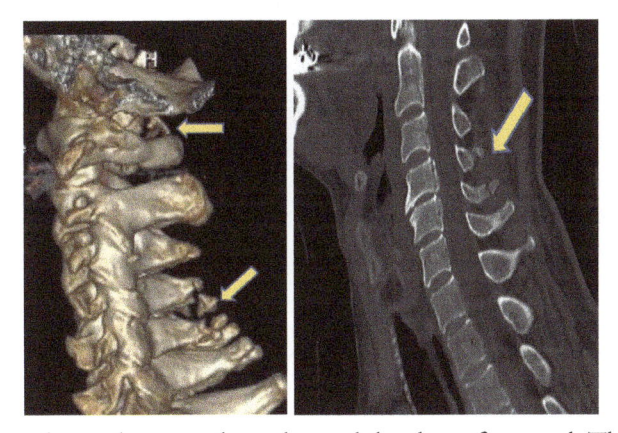

This image shows the area where the neck has been fractured. The picture on the left shows arrows pointing to the C1 fracture, and the C5 bone is completely separated. The photo to the right shows the fracture at C4.

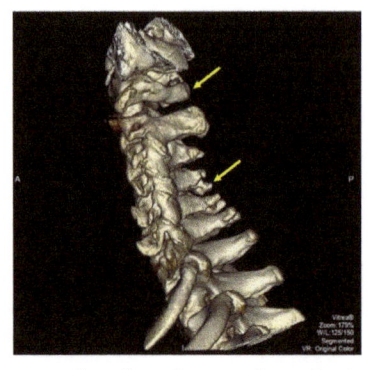

This MRI is seven months after the accident. It shows that the bones were completely reconnected and had no fractures. This is the miracle the doctors could not believe—how the bones reconnected without surgery.

The Study

Dr. Goldberg had a class of surgeons do a study with him on the internet. Before the actual study, he showed them my MRI and CT scan from the accident. He explained that I was a sixty-five-year-old man involved in a motorcycle accident. Looking at the MRI, there was strong evidence of a severe injury, and there was bleeding at the C1 vertebrae. He asked each of the surgeons, "What do you think was the result of this injury?" Ninety percent of the surgeons said that the subject died. The remaining ten percent said that the subject was paralyzed. They were all amazed that I survived the accident and even more surprised that I was healed without surgery. The study was to educate the surgeons on investigating the details of the person before rushing to surgery. Find out the person's health practices and treat each injury differently.

The study used the name Nicholas Giovanni. The study displayed the hospital records, complete details of the injury, and pictures of the fractured vertebrae. Displayed are MRIs showing the fracture and the final MRI with the neck bone reconnected without surgery.

The patient, Nicholas Giovanni (Dominick Giacobbe), is a sixty-year-old male who presented six months ago after a motorcycle collision. At that time, CT/MRI imaging found a C4-C5 spinous process fracture and C1 lateral mass extending to a transverse process fracture without mention of spinal cord injury, and the right vertebral artery was in close proximity to the fracture through the right lateral process of C1. Nontraumatic intracerebral subarachnoid hemorrhage was not noted but not ruled out. He declined pain medication about twelve hours after admission and was mobile and ambulating by twenty-four hours after admission. He refused the recommended ORIF surgery or halo fixation and was released about ninety-six hours after admission with instructions to wear the collar at all times and limit activity. Since then, he has been seen as an outpatient for imaging procedures. He had been showing progressive healing and removed his collar about three months after admission with instructions to limit physical activity. The patient appeared well developed and well nourished. His lab values and vitals were within the normal range. His demeanor was pleasant and cooperative, with a normal affect. A musculoskeletal exam revealed normal bulk and tone throughout, full ROM, and motor strength of 5/5 in the upper and lower extremities. CT/MRI scans demonstrated interval bony bridging of the right C1 transverse process fracture, with persistent narrowing of the vertebral artery foramen, although there was interval healing of the fracture. The progressive healing of the C4 and C5 spinous process fractures was also noted. Nicholas seemed to have recovered from his injuries to an extent sufficient to assume unrestricted activities. The collar was no longer needed. He could resume martial arts practice, which had been his main concern since the time of his injury.

In the study, the name Nicholas Giovanni was used.

The patient, Nicholas Giovanni, is a 65-year-old male who presented after crashing his motorcycle while wearing a helmet. He is wearing a C collar. He is awake, alert, and oriented to name, place, and person. Blood was noted in the mouth, and a right upper tooth is missing. He claims that he was going approximately 40 mph when a car pulled out in front of him. He was unable to lay his bike down, and he struck the back of the car with his face. He estimates that he lost consciousness (LOC) for about 5 minutes after the accident. Bruising is noted over his left shoulder, and he reports left shoulder pain. He also reports neck pain but denies abdominal pain and headaches. He described the pain as sharp, constant, nonradiating, and a 6/10 after medication (50 mcg fentanyl PF intravenous injection PRN). Functionally, the patient is independent with daily activities and ambulates independently prior to admission. He does not complain of radicular symptoms, including numbness or weakness. The patient denies loss of control of either bowel or bladder function. The patient had a tonsillectomy about 50 years ago, denies past or present tobacco use, and admits to occasional alcohol use. The patient denies allergies. The patient was logrolled with C-spine precautions. FAST (facial drooping, arm weakness, speech difficulties, and time) are negative with a Glasgow Coma Scale of 15. The patient appears well-developed and well-nourished, with a height and weight of 1.702 m (5'7"), 77.111 kg (170 lbs.), and a BMI of 26.62 kg/m^2. His lab values, including protime-INR and PTT, are normal. The vital signs are normal: pulse 70 bpm, blood pressure 131/77 mm Hg, temperature 98.2°F (36.8°C), respiratory rate 12 bpm, and SpO2 97%. He has a C-collar in place.

His demeanor is pleasant and cooperative, with a normal affect. ROS are all normal, aside from neck and shoulder pain, ecchymosis below the left eye and forehead, dried blood in the mouth, and a missing front tooth. His hearing is intact to a light whisper, and mucus membranes are moist. PERRLA is normal without a scleral icterus. A musculoskeletal exam reveals normal bulk and tone throughout, full ROM, and motor strength of 5/5 in the upper and lower extremities, with the exception of the left deltoid due to injury. Reflexes are normal without Hoffman's or Babinski's sign. Sensory intact to light touch shows cranial nerves II–XII intact, but unable to test drift due to left shoulder injury. He has limited range of motion of the left shoulder, right wrist ecchymosis, and abrasion over the second MCP joint, but no deformity is seen. CT/MRI scans demonstrate a C4-C5 spinous process fracture and a C1 lateral mass extending to a transverse process fracture without mention of spinal cord injury. Imaging shows no evidence of other acute osseous abnormalities, pneumothorax, hemorrhage, infarct, or mass. The CTA neck shows no involvement of vessels, but the right vertebral artery is in close proximity to the fracture through the right lateral process of C1.

Nontraumatic intracerebral subarachnoid hemorrhage is not noted but is not ruled out. Administered 2 mg intravenous morphine q4H PRN. Inner lower lip laceration (3 cm) was repaired with 4 interrupted sutures with lidocaine, followed by 15 mL of 0.12% chlorhexidine gluconate swish and spit q6H. Neomycin-bacitracin polymyxin was applied to abrasions q8H. Administered 50 mg Senokot/100 mg docusate oral BID/PRN, 30 mg enoxaparin by subcutaneous injection q12H, and 650 mg acetaminophen oral q6H. Nicholas declined oxycodone or other pain medication about 12 hours after admission (which made him feel "high and weird"). He was using an ice pack to help with pain. He was mobile and ambulating around the building by 24 hours after admission. The patient was educated about the dangers related to CHI/concussions but refused the recommended ORIF surgery or halo fixation. He was released into the care of his significant other 48 hours after admission after learning how to take his collar on and off. He was instructed to continue local wound care and wear the collar at all times with decreased activity. He will be seen in 4–6 weeks as an outpatient for new imaging and assessment.

T imaging axial, sagittal, and coronal images were obtained from the skull base to the thoracic inlet. Fracture seen through the right posterior body of C1 with extension through the superior aspect of the vertebral artery foramen, through the right transverse process of the Cl vertebral body, and through the C4 and C5 spinous processes. The C5 spinous process fracture extends through the shaft of the right C5 lamina, with extension through the medial aspect of the posterior component of the lamina on the right as well. The vertebral bodies are normally aligned, and body heights are preserved.

CT Imaging Technique: Axial images were obtained from the skull base to the thoracic inlet. Sagittal and coronal reformatted images were generated and reviewed. Automated dose-control measures were utilized. 3D post-processed images were obtained and reviewed. Findings: There is a straightening of the upper cervical lordosis. There is loss of height at the C4-5 disc space level and, to a lesser degree, C5-6 with an anterior osteophyte at C4-5. The vertebral body height and disc space heights are preserved. There has been interval healing of a right transverse process fracture of C1 with bony bridging. There is persistent narrowing of the right vertebral artery foramen. There is interval bony bridging of the C4 and C5 spinous process fractures. No focal, suspicious osseous lesion is identified. Paravertebral soft tissues are unremarkable. Visualized portions of the brain and calvarium are unremarkable. The visualized lung apices are clear.

Conclusions

1. Interval bony bridging of the right C1 transverse process fracture. There is a persistent narrowing of the vertebral artery foramen, although there is interval healing of the fracture.
2. Progressive healing of the C4 and C5 spinous process fractures relative to the prior study.
3. Degenerative changes occur with degenerative disc desiccation at C4-5 and, to a lesser degree, at C5-6. Uncovertebral joint hypertrophy with foraminal narrowing, as described above, is noted.

Angiography Report

The angiography-radiology CTA of the neck vessels finds no evidence of injury or stenosis involving the origins of the great vessels arising from the aortic arch. There is bilateral patency of the vertebral arteries throughout their course. The vertebral arteries are codominant in size. There is no evidence of injury or stenosis of either vertebral artery along its course. However, the right vertebral artery is in close proximity to the fracture through the right lateral process of C1. There is an unremarkable appearance to both common carotid arteries, both carotid bifurcations, and the origins of each internal and external carotid artery. Both internal carotid arteries distal to their origin are normal in appearance without evidence of stenosis or injury.

Chapter 7

Life after a Near-Death Experience

Life after a near-death experience changes you in many ways. One part of you is very appreciative, and the other part of you feels like you are Superman. Having the confidence to be able to have a normal life and not have the worries of being in a wheelchair is great. You become overwhelmed with appreciation for a healthy life. It's like being reborn and having an amazing feeling of true happiness. I have always been appreciative of all the great things in my life, but this is by far the best. Not only did I escape death and the chance of being paralyzed, but I am 100 percent healed and have no worries about reinjuring myself. However, my journey was not over. When you get a spinal cord injury, there are many changes that accrue. The one thing I noticed was an effect on my balance and coordination.

When I returned to karate training, I had new challenges to overcome. When I did a kick, I felt very uncoordinated and unnatural in my movements. When I did a spinning kick, my accuracy was off. I was now determined to get everything back to where it was before the injury. Right away, I began running. My endurance was not too bad, but my knees and ankles were very weak. After a few days of running, I strained the patella tendon in front of my knee. This was very painful, and I now had to work on healing that. The patella tendon connects your shin muscle to the kneecap, and when you hurt that, it develops extreme pain in the front of the knee when walking. I had to get a special brace and ice it continually till I got it to the point where I could resume full exercise. This injury lasted for about six weeks.

Besides teaching karate, I also teach boxing classes with a full go-ahead on my training. I was now allowed to punch the heavy bag. I did not punch the heavy bag for seven months. The doctor was worried that when hitting the bag, I would jolt my neck, and it could cause additional problems. Punching the bag was difficult at first, but as the days went on, I got stronger and stronger. At first, I had slight pain in my neck when punching the bag, but after a few weeks, the pain was gone. I began doing several balance exercises, trying to improve my balance issues. This was a very slow process of redeveloping balance. Whenever I did an exercise, I would lose my balance. This was very weird because all my life, I had amazing balance, and now I was struggling with simple things like standing with one leg up. I worked very hard on my balance, but I was not making any fast improvements. However, I was very determined to get back to where I was in the past.

My fitness routines kept increasing my strength and endurance. I was feeling stronger every day, but I was still not where I wanted to be. I remember starting on the bench press. Each week, four or five of my students meet for a chest workout. I had not done the workout in eight months, and I was now ready to start again. The last time I did the workout, I was able to bench press 185 lbs. ten times on my fifth set of bench presses. That was very good since my body weight was only 165 lbs. When I started, I was only able to do the bar, which was 45 lbs. I lost a lot of strength and coordination while lifting. However, in the next few weeks, I continued to increase the weights, and I was back to my original strength. It took about six months to get full strength back. I was very lucky; considering the extent of my injury, I have no physical pain. I slept well and woke up with no stiffness in my neck. I did notice tightness when I tilted my neck back and tried to look up, but there was no pain. The doctor told me that I might have pain in my neck for the rest of my life, but so far, there has been no pain.

When August came, exactly one year after the injury, I was feeling great. I remember getting the amazing feeling of being 100 percent normal. I was feeling very good about myself, and I was feeling very positive. The only issue I was dealing with was my balance and accuracy when performing my karate moves. I would have a student hold a pad, I would do a spinning kick, and for some reason, my kicks would not be where I wanted them to be. However, after a few months of continued work, I got my accuracy and balance back. It had been about a year and a half since the injury. I could say that I was back 100 percent.

I also had a new feeling of spiritual bonding with God. After going through an experience like I did, I truly realized that there is a God, and he is there when you need him. He comes to you in ways that cannot be explained. The injury I had did not heal the way I healed, and I was sure that God helped in my healing process. I prayed every day, and my prayers were answered with an amazing total healing. I prayed to Padre Pio and to Jesus, and I believe my prayers were answered. I now feel enlightened by the power of God, and I will forever be loyal to him. When you pray from your heart, your prayers will be answered. I do not want to believe that I am a superhuman. Rather, I believe that I am a person who asked for God's help and received it. I still pray each day that I stay pain-free and that I can maintain a long and healthy life. I will be there to help others, and I will give myself to God's light.

The accident did not enlighten me about God. I grew up Catholic and attended church regularly. My family believed in God, and I was taught to pray at a young age. However, I never knew of anybody's prayers being answered. Well, mine were answered. I will always try to be good, honest, and sincere, and I will always try to do everything in my life with God in my heart. My suggestion to everyone is that if you need a miracle, pray to God, and hopefully he will send you that miracle. All the time, people say to me that God blesses me. Well, I was blessed.

The other feeling you get after having a near-death experience, as I had, is a feeling that you are Superman. Yes, you honestly feel like you can walk through fire, or you can walk in front of a car, get hit, and survive. You get a strange feeling of being indestructible and a feeling of being a man of superpowers. It is funny how confidence is developed after tragedy accrues. When it happens, you feel weak and vulnerable, but when you conquer it, you feel powerful and confident. The feeling is strong and powerful, which propels you forward in life. It takes away all your fears. You truly believe that you have unseen powers and that you cannot be conquered. I think it's a feeling a warrior gets after he overcomes any life-threatening experience. If he never had an injury of this magnitude, he is always afraid and carries an internal weakness, but the warrior who had a serious injury and overcame it becomes the true fearless warrior. I truly feel like a fearless warrior.

I remember one time seeing an interview with a man who was struck by lightning and survived. The man spoke about his near-death experience, and he explained how he felt so powerful and felt that he was stronger than death. I do not know if it's the result of the experience or if it's just what happens when you come so close to death. I think all people fear death, but when you get too close to it, you realize that there is nothing to fear. I was wondering how many people have this kind of experience. I personally feel that very few people have had near-death experiences in their lifetime. It is like I already faced death, and I did not die, so now I have no fear of dying. You become strong when you eliminate fear. When you fear something, you are taught to face it to overcome it. Well, when you come close to death, you face death, and your fear of death is then gone. I feel great now, physically, mentally, and spiritually. I feel strong and healthy now, ready to face anything life may put in front of me.

> Anyone can quit or run away from their problems, but it is the person with true courage who will stand there and find a way to conquer their battles. They display true strength. (D. A. Giacobbe)

Chapter 8

Conclusion

In conclusion, I would like to thank God, my family, and all my students and friends who have supported me through this horrifying and fearful experience. I have grown stronger from it, and I now believe in miracles. About a year and a half after my accident, I visited my doctor. All the nurses and workers said, "Oh, here is the miracle man!"

I smiled and thought, *Yes, it is a miracle that I am fine after this near-death experience.*

My doctor shook my hand and said, "I am happy that you overcame your injuries. You are a very lucky man. It is a miracle that you are not paralyzed."

I thought, *Yes, it is a miracle, and I appreciate being healthy again.* I am now completely healed and back teaching three to four classes a day of *Tang Soo Do* Korean karate, boxing, and fitness classes. I overcame all the problems related to my injury. I have no pain, and I sleep well. I am happy to be alive and happier that I can continue being an active karate master. My message to the world is that miracles do happen, but you must work hard with them. It was a miracle that I did not die upon contact. It was a miracle that I was not paralyzed instantly after the accident, but everything after that was about using all my strength and determination to heal and be back to normal. I never had a negative attitude. I was confident that I was going to conquer this obstacle. Even when the doctor was feeding me many negative thoughts, I stayed positive. Deep down inside my heart, I knew I was going to be okay. I thought of it as a roadblock, and I was not going to let the roadblock stop my journey through life. I am now stronger from this experience, and I am now more appreciative of God, my family, friends, and my life. In life, we will always be faced with battles. Be sure to face your battles and never give up the fight. I will never forget any of the details, nor will I ever forget all the pain and suffering I had to go through. There is an old saying: "What doesn't kill us makes us stronger."

Upon the completion of this book, it is four years after the accident. I am completely healed and back to 100 percent. I have no pain or stiffness in my neck at all. It is like I never had an injury. I have redeveloped my balance and flexibility. I feel strong and injury-free. I am very happy that I can continue to have the life I have, and I appreciate all the people who supported me through this long journey.

These pictures were taken in Ireland after teaching a three-hour seminar two years after the accident. I was demonstrating *Tang Soo Do* karate techniques.

Tang Soo Do side kick

DOMINICK GIACOBBE

Grand Master Giacobbe performing a jumping side kick

Full balance and power redeveloped after two years of hard work

OVERCOME

Performing *Tang Soo Do* moves with power and no pain

Special thanks to Angela. She was amazing—better than a nurse.

DOMINICK GIACOBBE

I have great appreciation and love for my sister, Master Barbara Giacobbe. She is the spirit of love.

Thank you, Grand Master Don Straga. Your support and dedication helped me through this challenge.

Each stream finds its way to a river. Each river finds its way to the ocean. In life, we must always flow and find our way to bigger and better things. Reach for the stars, and you will touch them.(D. A. Giacobbe)

OVERCOME

My Seven Miracles or Near-Death Experiences in My Life

My Seven Miracles

I am the survivor of seven miracles—seven impossible experiences, or should I say seven near-death experiences in my life. Do I have an angel following me, or am I just a lucky man? How many near-death experiences can a person have in one lifetime? I personally believe that luck has not been my protector. I think God and faith have given me an angel who is with me and who has helped me survive the unbelievable. In this book, I take you on my journey through how I fractured my neck and how I completely healed from it. It is the journey of overcoming the impossible.

My First Miracle

My first miracle was when I was about two years old. We lived in Brooklyn, New York, in a project on the second floor. It was a hot evening in the summer. My father was home, taking care of myself and my two brothers. My mother went out to the movies with her sister. My father was a hard worker. At the time, he was working three jobs. He was extremely tired and told my mom to go to the movies, and he would stay home with us. It was early evening. He put us to bed, and he lay down on the couch and fell asleep. I happened to get out of bed and work my way into the living room since it was a very hot evening and we had no air conditioning in the apartment. The window was open for air. As a very active child, I climbed onto the window and put one leg out and the other inside. I was straddling the window as if I were riding a horse. Soon, a crowd gathered and saw a little kid by the window. The people in the crowd began to panic, waiting to see what was going to happen. One person tried to knock on the apartment door, but my dad was in a deep sleep because he was exhausted from his very rigorous work schedule. Because it was a heavy metal door, it was hard to make enough noise to wake him up. One of the teenagers went to the next-door apartment, climbed across the window, and rescued me. It was a frightening experience for my parents. I unknowingly experienced my first miracle.

My Second Miracle

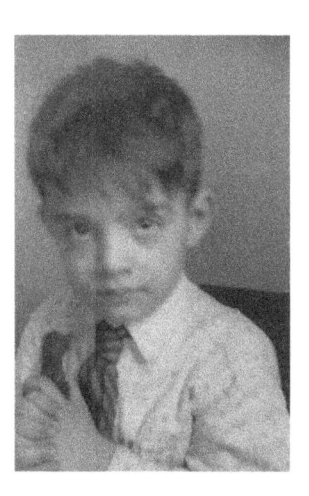

My second miracle was when I was about seven or eight years old. I had a knot in the shoelace of my shoe. As a young boy, I figured I would cut the shoelace so I could get the shoe onto my foot. I took a knife out of the drawer, sat on the kitchen chair, placed the shoe between my legs, took the knife, and put it between the shoelace where the knot was. I then pulled on the knife with both hands really hard. Not being aware of my situation, the knife cut through the shoelace and stabbed me right in the throat. My mom was in the next room and screamed in fear. I was yelling help with a knife sticking out of my throat. My mom ran downstairs for help. There was a gang of teenagers standing there. She screamed for their help. They all ran up the steps, picked me up, and made a human stretcher. I was lying flat on the shoulders of five or six teenagers. They ran four blocks to the hospital. My mom was in a panic. There was blood running down my chest. Everyone thought I was going to die.

It was funny. Although everyone was in a panic, I was calm and had a feeling of protection and a strong feeling that I was fine and that I was going to be okay. We got to the hospital, and they rushed me into the emergency room. The knife was still in my neck. Nobody wanted to touch it. The doctors took some X-rays, cleaned the area, and slowly pulled the knife out of my neck. They put a few stitches into my neck and said that I was going to be okay. The doctor told my mom that I was a lucky boy and that if the knife went a quarter of an inch either way, it would have been fatal. My mom was very upset but relieved, knowing that I was going to be okay. I was not upset or scared. I had a feeling of confidence that I was going to be fine and that there was nothing to worry about. I survived my second near-death experience, but this time, I was old enough to remember the experience of danger and fear.

My Third Miracle

My third miracle came when I was about eleven or twelve years old. My father asked me to go to the store to pick up something for him. It was a Saturday afternoon. The walk to the candy store was five blocks. Along the way, there was the school. It was a huge school with a large cement yard and a high fence all the way around. It was a shortcut to go through the school yard to get to the store. As I was going through the yard, there were eight of nine older guys, the tough guys. In New York, at that time, there were many gangs and groups of tough kids. As I approached the guys, they began bullying me. One pushed me, and it kept escalating. I tried to walk through them, but they pulled me back. Soon they were smacking me, and then I got a punch in the stomach. I fell to my knees. They were all laughing, and I jumped up and tried to make a run for it. They quickly grabbed me and pulled me to the school's lower window.

This was really old-school. On the lower windows were bars to prevent anyone from breaking into the school. On one of the window bars was a metal wire trash can attached to the bar with a chain on the top and a chain on the bottom. The guys dragged me to the trash can. I was unable to move. They were all holding me down. They then put my head against the bar and pulled the trash can over my head. I was now pinned to the bar with the trash can against my neck. It was so tight that as they rolled the trash can across my face, my tooth pierced my face. My face was bleeding. I was unable to move because my hands were behind me. I was on my knees. The guys all ran away, leaving me there. I tried to yell for help, but the nearest house was really far away. I felt sacred at first, but then that feeling came over me that I was going to be okay. I felt protected, and I was calm and just concentrated on my breathing.

I was there for over an hour before somebody discovered me. They tried to get me out, but it was impossible. I had lots of blood running from my cheek and was feeling weak. The man ran to a nearby house, and they called the police. He came back with a towel and held it on my face to stop the bleeding. The police arrived, and they could also not get me out of the hold I was in. The policeman then called the fire company, and a big fire engine arrived. They had to hacksaw the chain to get me out. I was again rushed to the hospital in the police car. I had received stitches inside my mouth and on my cheek. Everyone was so upset and said that it was a good thing that man found me, or I could have died being pinned there and bleeding. However, I was again calm during the whole episode. The same feeling I had earlier in my life was present. I felt protected and safe. I survived my third miracle.

OVERCOME

My Fourth Miracle

That's me in the center with the guitar, hanging out with the kids on the block in New York City.

My fourth miracle came when I was fourteen years old. I was in high school on the lunch line. One of the older kids from high school budded in front of me on the lunch line. I told the guy, "Hey, go to the end of the line." He was older and began acting very arrogant and aggressive. I knew it was escalating, and I was thinking that I was going to have to fight this guy. Suddenly, he pushed me. I fell back about five feet. I reacted by running at him, and I pushed him hard. He went back about ten feet, fell over a chair, and knocked somebody's books over. While he was on the floor, he was fiddling around and then jumped up and attacked me. As I was hitting him in the face, he hit me in the stomach very hard. I just kept punching him, and within a few seconds, the teachers ran over and broke up the fight.

To my surprise and that of everyone else there, my white shirt had a huge red blood stain. Not knowing it during the fight, I was stabbed in the stomach with a compass. It went deep into my stomach, and the bleeding was not stopping. The teachers called the ambulance, and again, I was rushed to the hospital. Again, everyone around me was crying and very scared. They thought I was going to die. But I was calm, and that same feeling of calmness overwhelmed me. I knew I was going to be okay. In the hospital, the doctors did some tests, and I had to stay for the night. The doctors told my mother and father that I was very lucky that the stab wound just missed my organs and that I would just be sore for a few weeks. I just escaped my fourth near-death experience. The doctor said it's a miracle that the stab missed everything and that I had no internal bleeding. Again, I knew that I was going to be okay. I had that confident feeling of being protected, a feeling of being safe, even though it could have been a very serious situation.

My Fifth Miracle

My fifth miracle was surviving a very serious auto accident. I was driving my car down a country road in New Jersey. I was eighteen years old on my way to college. As I approached an intersection, I had the right of way. I was traveling around fifty miles per hour when another vehicle came to the intersection. He was supposed to stop, but he did not see the stop sign and ran into the left side of my car, right on my door. He was going over fifty miles per hour. As soon as I saw his car approach, it was like it was happening in slow motion. I took my left arm and placed it on the side of my face. I held the steering wheel tightly with my left hand. There was a loud crashing sound, and the glass flew all over the car. My car was pushed off the road to the right, and I hit a telephone poll. It was a very serious accident. My car was crushed like an accordion. All the windows were blown out, and I was pinned in the car. The front seat, which was supposed to seat two people, was now reduced to one seat. I was sitting there in the car with no room to move. My legs were pinned in, and my shoulders were touching both sides of the car.

As I sat there, I realized how bad the accident was, but I saw that I was not hurt; although all the windows were blown out, I did not have a cut. I felt a bit dazed by the impact, but I had that same feeling of safety that came over me in the past. I had the feeling that I was protected and that I was going to be okay. I could not open either door. On one side was a telephone poll, and on the other side was the other car. I heard the man in the other vehicle crying. He thought he killed me. I said to the man, "I'm okay."

He said, "Oh, my God! I'm sorry."

I then wiggled my legs out and crawled out of the car through the front window. In those days, we didn't wear seat belts, so in the accident, I hit my back on the opposite side of the car, and that was the only pain I felt. Within a few minutes, the police arrived. They said, "Is somebody in the car?"

I said, "No, sir. I was the driver."

The policeman said, "No way! You don't have any scratches."

I said, "I'm okay."

He said, "Listen, son, you don't go through an accident like that and not get an injury. I'm calling the ambulance and getting you to the hospital."

The other driver was bleeding from his head and had to be put on a stretcher. I went to the hospital. They ran some tests on me and found blood in my urine. They said that this was very serious and that I had a bruised kidney. I would have to stay in the hospital to be treated. It could cause kidney failure, and I could die. I told the doctors that I would be okay. After five days in the hospital, the blood stopped appearing in my urine, and I was released. When I saw my car, I realized how it was a miracle that I wasn't killed in the crash.

My Sixth Miracle

My sixth miracle was a very scary one. I was on my motorcycle in Florida. It was late at night. I was riding the motorcycle from Fort Lauderdale to West Palm Beach when my motorcycle engine blew a gasket. I had to stop and pull to the side of the road. Not knowing the area, I figured I would sleep at the side of the bike till morning, then figure out how I could get to a repair shop. I was down in Florida for a temporary construction job. I fell asleep alongside my bike. I was suddenly awakened by a man kicking me. I jumped up, and I noticed that I was surrounded by seven biker gang members. They saw the motorcycle, but they didn't see me because I was sleeping. They had a white van and began harassing and questioning me.

At that point in my life, I was a red belt in karate and had been training in karate for about three years. As the conversation was getting worse, one of the guys pulled out a huge hunting knife, came over to me, and put it close to my throat. I said, "Hey, back off! There's no issue here."

They kept asking me if I was in a biker gang. I kept saying, "No, I just broke down and was waiting for help to arrive." Suddenly, one of the guys kicked at me in the groin. Using what I learned from my karate training, I grabbed his legs. The second guy had a handgun behind his back and hit me on the face, breaking my nose and knocking one of my front teeth out. However, after the impact, I held the guy's leg so hard that I flipped him to the ground. There was a slight hesitation because they expected me to be knocked out. As the guy lifted his arm with the gun to hit me again, I gave him a roundhouse karate kick, knocking him back. The big guy with the knife started coming after me. I just kept moving, pushing guys into each other, and I just kept trying to hit whoever I could.

At one instant, a guy grabbed me from behind and stuck a gun in my back while he was choking me. I quickly spun around and knocked the gun out of his hand with my elbow. I saw the gun on the ground and went for it, but two of the guys pulled me away just as my hand touched the gun. It was so insane. Things were happening so fast, but I was just trying to fight my way to safety. Suddenly, there was a separation. I was walking backward, and they were all walking toward me. The problem was that I was backing up and going farther from the highway. As I went backward, I slid down an embankment, which was now in chest-deep everglades water. Before I could get out, three guns were pointed at me. The gang leader said to the other guys, "Get out of here! I'm taking this guy out!"

I stood there in the water and said to myself that I wasn't going to beg for my life. If he was going to shoot me, then I was going to just stand there. At one point, I thought I should dive in the water, but I knew he would shoot me for sure. As I looked into the barrel of the gun, I got the feeling again that I was protected. As soon as I got that feeling, the guy put the gun down and said, "I'm going to let you live. Don't come out of the water, or I will kill you." He then ran off, and they took my motorcycle. I tried to get out of the water as soon as possible to see their license plate, but it was too late. They were pulling onto the highway.

    I ran out onto the highway, stopped a car, and begged them to give me a ride. I got a ride to the next exit and contacted the police. They told me that I was a lucky man and that these gangs usually just shoot their victims. I sat there with the police, realizing how lucky I was to be alive. This was a really close-to-death experience. I kept thinking about why he wouldn't just kill me. Was it because my angel stopped him, or was it because I showed courage and fought back? I thought about that for years. However, the bad experience motivated me to return to my karate training with a purpose. I said to myself, *This will never happen again. If I ever get into another conflict, my kicks and punches will be so powerful that no human will be able to conquer me.* This determination led me to become successful in competitions, and it led me to open a karate school and have a very successful life in martial arts. I survived my sixth miracle.

My Seventh Miracle

On a bike ride through the New York State area with Angela and karate student Keith Bennett

Miracle number seven. I was involved in a very serious, near-death motorcycle accident in which I fractured my neck in three places. I was traveling fifty miles per hour on a country road in New Jersey on my Harley-Davidson Fat Boy motorcycle when a car suddenly pulled out into my lane, blocking the road. It all happened so fast that I could not avoid the vehicle. I crashed directly into the side of his car. I hit the car straight on, contacting my face and head to the side of the car. In the crash, I fractured my neck, bruised my ribs, injured my shoulder, lost two teeth, and had numerous cuts and scratches on my face. Ninety-nine percent of people who fracture the C1 vertebra of the neck either die or are totally paralyzed. I fractured C1 in three places, and I also fractured C4 and C5. As the doctors explained to me, fracturing C1 is the worst injury a human can have. Surviving an accident of this magnitude is a miracle. In life, we always hear of miracles but never believe that you may be one of them.

I am, by trade, a karate teacher, a grand master of the martial arts, a fifty-year student of *Tang Soo Do* Korean karate, a meditation practitioner, and a student of tai chi and chi healing. I was confronted with a very serious injury that threatened my ability to continue my practice of martial arts. In this book, I will explain how I survived the accident and how I overcame the serious neck injury through positive thinking, visual meditation, chi healing, tai chi, fitness training, internal breathing exercises, and the will to survive. Miracles do happen, and I am a true example of that. However, it is also possible to make miracles happen through the power of mental determination. In this book, I will take you on my journey toward making a miracle. I hope my experiences motivate others to overcome the odds and develop a never-quit attitude for whatever they may be faced with. It all starts with your mind and with the thoughts you supply to your brain. The power of positive thinking and mental power is undeniable. We all possess minds. However, very few people actually use the power of their minds to overcome obstacles they may encounter in life. Life is a miracle, and surviving life is also a miracle. Miracles do happen. I am proof of that.

Never give up on your dreams. Never give up on yourself, and never allow negativity to discourage you. You can conquer anything you are faced with. You have the power. (D. A. Giacobbe)

About the Author

Grand Master Dominick A. Giacobbe, the holder of a ninth dan black belt in the two-thousand-year-old art of *Tang Soo Do* Korean karate, began his study of karate in 1968 under Grand Master J. C. Shin, who is well known for teaching the karate movie star Chuck Norris. Master Shin personally trained Mr. Giacobbe.

In the late '60s and early '70s, Master Giacobbe gained a reputation as a top tournament competitor on the East Coast. In 1974, Master Giacobbe opened the Tang Soo Karate Academy in Blackwood, New Jersey. His academy is one of the largest karate schools in the USA. In 1977, he traveled to Korea to fine-tune his art and learned the ancient techniques of mind power, derived from internal chi energy. His skills in developing mind power through meditation and special breathing exercises have set him apart from all other martial artists. Master Giacobbe has appeared numerous times on TV, showing his unbelievable demonstrations of *Tang Soo Do* mind power, in which he pierces his arms with sharpened motorcycle spokes, hangs buckets of water, and demonstrates this with no blood and no *pain*. He amazed audiences on *Guinness World Records, Incredible Sunday, That's Incredible, Evening Magazine, Good Morning America, Sally Jessie Raphael, CNN, After Hours, Entertainment Tonight*, and several other national TV shows.

His expertise has been used for the training of many professional athletes. In 1980, members of the Philadelphia Eagle football team began training with Master Giacobbe to enhance their skills in football. In 1987, Coach Buddy Ryan assigned the entire Philadelphia Eagles defense to train off-season with Master Giacobbe. For five years, the Eagles defense was the best in the league. Mr. Giacobbe personally trained NFL stars Reggie White and Mike Quick. He was also the special physical trainer for many world champion boxers, working on fifteen world championship bouts. Master Giacobbe personally trained Evander Holyfield, Pernell Whitaker, and Sugar Ray Leonard for several of their championship fights. Master Giacobbe has also appeared on the covers of six martial arts magazines, including *Black Belt Magazine* and *Karate Kung Fu Illustrated*. His expertise in karate has been the subject of many international magazine stories. In 1985, he won a gold medal in Japan at the World Super People Festival. Master Giacobbe amazed the Japanese judges, standing atop authentic razor-sharp Japanese samurai swords without getting cut.

The governor of New Jersey has also awarded Master Giacobbe for his juvenile offender program. The program took troubled juveniles and put them into karate training. All the kids had positive results. In 1983, Master Giacobbe was presented the Excalibur Award from the American Cancer Society for his donation of over $600,000 from the Fight for Cancer National Karate Championships, which he sponsors in Atlantic City annually.

In the year 2000, Master Giacobbe was inducted into the Black Belt Magazine Hall of Fame. This is the highest honor a martial artist can achieve. He shares this honor with Bruce Lee, Jackie Chan, and Chuck Norris.

Grand Master Giacobbe, the president of the Intercontinental Tang Soo Do Organization (ITO), teaches seminars around the world. His seminars include the traditional teachings of *Tang Soo Do* Korean karate, martial arts philosophy, meditation, chi breathing exercises, and chi meditation for healing. Master Giacobbe personally teaches at the Tang Soo Karate Academy in Voorhees, New Jersey.

Here Grand Master D. A. Giacobbe is performing mind over matter with sharpened motorcycle spokes pierced through his arms, hanging buckets of water, and standing on razor-sharp swords.

Since the fractured neck, Grand Master Dominick Giacobbe has been living a strong, healthy life. He experiences no pain or discomfort from the injury. The fracture is completely healed.

Dominick has lived an amazing life with hundreds of accomplishments and awards. He defies defeat with the power of his mind. His determination and dedication have made him a leader of men and women.

The ability to overcome whatever you are faced with is at the core of his philosophy.

Presently, Master Giacobe teaches motivational seminars around the world. He conducts seminars on motivation, mind power, meditation, *Tang Soo Do* Korean karate, self-defense, health, and fitness. For information on having Master Giacobbe do a seminar for your group, please contact him by email at dgiacobbe9@gmail.com.